MW00330279

THE STORY OF THE
LAFAYETTE ESCADRILLE

Portrait of the author, Captain Thenault,
commanding the Lafayette Escadrille.

The Story of the LaFayette Escadrille

TOLD BY ITS COMMANDER
CAPTAIN GEORGES THENAULT

TRANSLATED BY
WALTER DURANTY

WITH AN INTRODUCTION BY
ANDRE TARDIEU
High Commissioner of Franco-American Affairs

THE BATTERY PRESS
Nashville

Reprinted by
THE BATTERY PRESS
P.O. Box 3108, Uptown Station
Nashville, Tennessee 37219
Fifth in the Great War Series
1990
ISBN: 0-89839-148-2

Printed in the United States of America

To the Memory of

CHAPMAN,	HOSKIER,
ROCKWELL,	DE LAAGE, DE MEUX,
PRINCE,	MacMONAGLE,
MacCONNELL,	CAMPBELL,
GENET,	LUFBERY.
DRESSY,	

MY COMPANIONS IN ARMS,

A TRIBUTE OF SUPREME ADMIRATION.

G. T.

PREFACE

My dear Captain,

I accept with pleasure the task of introducing your fine book to the French and American public,—firstly because it gives me yet another opportunity of honoring the glorious dead and the heroic living of your gallant escadrille, and secondly because I wish myself to express the high esteem that I feel for you, its commander during nearly two years.

You have wished to put on record, for the enlightenment of new generations in France and America, the story of the volunteers who served under your orders and gave so noble a response to the deed of La Fayette, whom they chose as their namesake. More than a century apart, the great ancestor and your young Americans were inspired by the same passion of Liberty. It was your duty to bear witness to their exploits.

You have told this story of heroism with a

sincere simplicity which recommends it not only to literary critics but to all young people who take delight in noble deeds. To obtain this result all you needed was to tell what you had done and what you had seen.

The first American volunteers of your escadrille began their service in the Foreign Legion. They wished to fight to defend Liberty, which France incarnated and protected.

Some months later, as aviation developed, they were able to begin their training as pilots. In April, 1916, the creation of the American escadrille was decided, and from that moment this escadrille took part in every great action. During twenty-one months it was to be seen over every important battlefield.

First came Verdun, where you won your earliest glorious laurels with 146 fights and 13 enemy planes defeated. Then the Vosges, and the Somme—a period when the supremacy of allied aviation became manifest, a period of heroic combats, in which the Sioux, which you took as your emblem, won a terrible reputation in the enemy's ranks. It was then that you became the "LAFAYETTE ESCADRILLE."

In the United States the exploits of your escadrille had—I could see that for myself—a great
moral influence, and the example of your volunteers was an inspiration to many of their countrymen. We never doubted what America's decision would be; but since your pilots were the forerunners theirs will be the glory.

The war dragged on and you never rested. . . .
After the Somme came the battle of the Aisne,
then Flanders, then the return to Verdun where
you collaborated in the recapture of the Mort-
Homme and the Hill 304. A magnificent citation was the reward of your splendid efforts. I
desire to reproduce it here:

"Escadrille formed of American volunteers
come to fight for France in the purest spirit of
sacrifice, carried on without truce under the command of Captain Thenault a burning struggle
against our enemies.

"In very severe combats and at the price of
heavy losses, which far from weakening it only
raised its morale, brought down 28 enemy aeroplanes.

"Won the profound admiration of the Chiefs
who had it under their orders, and of the French

escadrilles which fighting beside it were spurred
to gallant rivalry."

That is a patent of nobility granted for ever
to those who survive as to those who have fallen,
to whom you piously dedicate your book: Prince,
Chapman, Rockwell, MacConnell, Genet, Dressy,
Hoskier, De Laage de Meux, MacMonagle,
Campbell, Lufbery!

Let us keep green in our hearts the memory
of these heroes. They loved France with the
same love that we feel for America, pure and
disinterested. They have taught us by their
willing sacrifice our common duty to maintain
and strengthen the union between the two great
peoples. They have shown the way, it is for us
to follow it. They died that a new world might
be born, it is for us to put into reality their glorious purpose.

To prepare this future, there is nothing so valuable as the knowledge of the past we have
shared. I thank you for having understood this
and for having given, by your book, to the two
fraternal Democracies, so splendid a reason for
better mutual esteem and mutual affection.

ANDRE TARDIEU.

INTRODUCTORY

This story of the Escadrille Lafayette is in no sense official—it is personal. I have not sought to give an account so much of what was accomplished in the air as of our intimacy—the life we led together and our surroundings in repose. I have refrained particularly from extolling any one above his comrades. Each played well his part. All made good.

To a few, like Norman Prince, Lufbery, Rockwell and Chapman, has fallen most of the honor of publicity, but they had the loyal support of the squadron in their exploits and to them came the glory of death. They gave their lives, as all were ready to do, but fate claimed them.

Those who were spared did their part as well as their temperament and opportunity permitted.

Some men are born-fighters:

> They who look beyond the night,
> They who see in dawn's pale light,
> One more day in which to fight—
> Those no death can stop.

The *gloria certaminis* is to such an inspiration and may be said to give an advantage over others, less gifted, in the contest, but they are not the less to be admired who went in on their nerve and pluck.

Fighting in the air requires the highest qualities of combat for in the fuller sense the aviator contends alone. He is not in touch with his commander or his comrades. He has not the influence of the close contact, the shoulder to shoulder morale that is found in the line of battle below him. The aviator flies in the deafening clamor of his motor; no word of warning or command can reach him. He cannot stand still. He is ever in motion at great speed. He must depend upon himself and above all upon his machine,—a delicate instrument and of limited flight. We were a fighting not a bombing squadron and our Nieuport de Chasses carried motive power for some two hours only.

Again aviation was a new science, a development of the war, and there was not a class of experienced men from which to draw. They had to learn the art under fire. They who went over the top on the battlefield were men trained to establish theories of war and led by professional experts in those theories.

The Aviators had no such advantage. They were trained to fly and but little more until experience evolved a system of attack and defense. Aviation was also the most dangerous of all the branches of the army for the machine itself was even more fatal than the guns of the Enemy. Besides, as a practical engine of war the real test of all new types was made at the front with all its accompanying risks.

I may say even that every aviator entered the service knowing that he was flying to his end— none faltered—all were volunteers. Honor to the heroes of America who joyfully devoted themselves to death for the great cause they represented.

A word as to the credit of originating the squadron. It belongs to Norman Prince, who first conceived the idea of bringing together his countrymen with some of those of the foreign legion in a squadron of flyers to be known as the Escuadrille Américaine. Cooperating with Prince were Cowden and Thaw. They were its founders and were always recognized as such, which gave them a certain prestige willingly accorded by the others in their mutual relations.

These three did not foresee that they were building better than they knew. Primarily their object was to serve France and beat the Boche. They loved France.

But the result of their endeavour was far reaching. Their example, their readiness to die for the cause they espoused and above all the glorious deaths of Chapman, Rockwell and Norman Prince—I follow the order of their fall—aroused their compatriots from the doubt of neutrality to a comprehension of the vital issues at stake—the safety of Liberty, the preservation of Democracy. The sacrifice of their young lives stirred their countrymen beyond all argument of words— theirs was the propaganda by deeds, and they won out.

Thus they were the precursors of that mighty awakening of the West,—of that gigantic effort of America—unparalleled in history—the greatest of all crusades—where every qualified fighting man was enrolled under the Stars and Stripes, for no selfish aim, for no world-conquest, but for the great ideals upon which civilization depends and for which the entire resources of the nation were unsparingly contributed to assure victory.

As I look back through the eyes of Memory on the eager, fearless, genial band that I had in charge—each so loyal, all so resolute, I think of those lines by the Bayard of Scottish Chivalry—Montrose—who died for his cause:

> "He either fears his fate too much
> Or his deserts are small
> That dares not put it to the touch
> To win or lose it all."

G. T.

My men so dared.

CONTENTS

CHAPTER I
PAGE

Origin of the Escadrille—The Foreign Legion—How
the idea of creating an American Escadrille arose .

CHAPTER II

Luxeuil—Captain Happe—Alsace—First flights—
First successes . . . .

CHAPTER III

Verdun—A Great Battle at its height—Chapman—
The Escadrille distinguishes itself . . . .

CHAPTER IV

PARIS

Life on leave—Return to Luxeuil—Kiffin Rockwell
—Norman Prince . . . .

CHAPTER V

The Somme—Cachy Wood—Amiens—Winter . .

CHAPTER VI

Spring and renewed activity—General advance—
Losses—Ham—Chaudun—Battle of the Aisne .

CONTENTS

CHAPTER VII

CHAPTER VIII

THE STORY OF THE
LAFAYETTE ESCADRILLE

THE LAFAYETTE ESCADRILLE

CHAPTER I

Origin of the Escadrille—The Foreign Legion—How the
Idea of creating an American Escadrille arose

The LaFayette Escadrille did not spring fully
armed into being. Its creation was a work of
difficulty and attended by no small delay.

When war broke out between France and Germany many were those who hurried from all
parts of the world to volunteer for the defence of
France.

Once again Germany was evidently the ag-
gressor and all those whose spirit urged them
towards justice had no hesitation as to which side
they should choose.

Naturally in a strong, healthy race like that
of the United States, with its hundred years of
sympathy for France, the adventurous nature
of the game to be played appealed to every one
who shared the American instinct for helping

the weak against the strong. In this case the weaker was France, with her population a third smaller and her armaments limited by a deliberately pacifist policy, face to face with Germany, the country of the *dry powder* and *the sharpened sword,* where each New Year saw the military budget formidably increased.

Among the Americans, first were naturally those who were already in France. But volunteering for the French army was no easy business, and proved enough to discourage the most determined will. Enquirers were sent from office to office; they were asked for papers and yet more papers, but they refused to be discouraged. They got their friends to act for them and finally their perseverance took the bureaucratic resistance by assault, and they managed to sign their engagement as volunteers at the Invalides, the very place where in 1792 the Parisians had come to volunteer when the country had been declared in danger and the National Assembly issued its call to arms.

Some of them tried to get into the aviation, like Norman Prince, Elliot Cowdin and William Thaw, already brilliant pilots. But that was out of the question; there were not enough machines for our own French pilots. We began the war with 80 machines. Moreover, everything foreign was regarded with a certain suspicion. Germany had organized her network of espionage so thoroughly that the French authorities at that time fancied they saw spies everywhere. They were afraid even of their best friends.

The only legal way for a foreigner to enter the French army was to join the Foreign Legion as a second-class soldier. If one was of age and of strong constitution no other conditions were needed.

What lay before them was the life of the foot-soldier, that is, the greatest risk, the lack of all comforts, a monotonous and wearisome existence, glory always hidden and limited, and, we may as well admit it, to pass one's life side by side— among brave and honest men—with some who were brave also but for whom the Legion had been a refuge from the justice of their country.

The future was not rosy, therefore, but in their fear of being too late, fear which maddened them against the apathy opposed to their desires, the Americans did not hesitate.

No matter what happened, no matter where it might be, they wanted to fight.

They all saw themselves already on the front, rifle in hand bringing down the Boche, the moment their engagement was signed. . . . Yet another disillusion. . . . What came next was the life in a training camp in the South of France, with weary marches on the dusty roads. The war was going to be a test of patience and endurance. The noblest spirit must be trained to endure even if it should lose some of its fire in the process.

Meanwhile on the front the Legion was doing its duty bravely at the price of heavy losses.

About the 15th of September, 1914, reinforcements were demanded from the depot to fill up the gaps in the ranks, to reinforce the old Legionaries, heroes of Africa and Tonkin.

The first choice was to fall on those who had seen previous service in any army. All our Americans came forward with long stories of imaginary campaigns in Mexico or the South American Republics.

The officer in charge of the depot asked at this time for volunteers to stay some months longer at

The Escadrille at full strength.   (30/4/16)

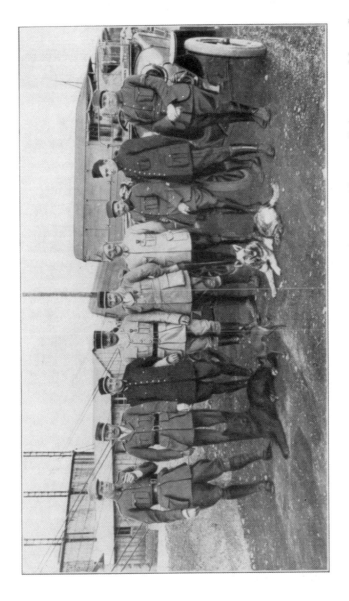

Chapman   Bert Hall   Capt. Thenault   Norman Prince   Mac   Connell

Cowdin   Thaw   De Laage de Meux   Rockwell

Different types of bombs dropped by aeroplanes.

the rear and take a further course of instruction with a view to becoming officers. All the Americans declined and at the beginning of October they all found themselves at the front in the sectors of Rheims and Craonnelle. Now for desperate bayonet charges against a gallant foe to the blast of the bugle; now for the battle to the death in which their skill, courage and strength were bound to triumph. . . . Yet another disillusion.

The soldier's life was not what our heroes imagined. Those were the days of organization when every one had to dig trenches, boyaux and shelters. Every night there was barbed wire to be put in position, and stakes to be hammered down with hammers muffled in rags, lest the everready mitrailleuse, "the devil's coffee mill," as the poilus called it, might begin to grind. Never an enemy to be seen except occasionally out of range through the shaky glass of a periscope.

For food they had to bring everything from three and a half miles in the rear, because the smoke of the kitchens made them only too easily spotted. This whole distance had to be traversed at night across country cut into ravines, in whose depths stagnant marshes lay hidden. Often the fatigue party upset their buckets falling head over heels over some obstacle, and the food that reached the first lines was always cold and generally mixed with mud. Once the battalion to which our Americans belonged tried to bring its kitchens up nearer. The Boche immediately spotted their smoke and that very evening twenty men were killed and wounded among their stoves by a single shell. They had to move them back again post-haste.

It was a hard life for our Americans. Winter became very severe from November; 25° of frost and no proper means of withstanding it; no warm shelters, no heavy clothes, not even straw. And they had to stay thirty days at a time in the front lines through lack of troops to relieve them.

It was war in all its misery, dirt and squalor. No means of getting clean, no water to wash in, all of them covered with vermin. Great courage and great discipline were needed to endure this hell, but Joffre had said at the Marne: "Die rather than retreat"; the watchword was still the same.

First of all they had to hold on. They held

on, and gradually, thanks to hard work, experience and ingenuity, conditions got better. These were the days when all the women in France from chateau to cottage set themselves to knit furiously, and gradually a supply of warm clothing began to reach the front.

The Americans were in a comparatively quiet sector, for at this period the limited production of munitions was only just enough for the storm centres, which then were concentrated around the Yser. So losses were not heavy and the first American wounded was Bouligny, by a shrapnel ball, in November.

The desperate monotony of trench life was only broken by incessant sentry-go at the lookout posts and by an occasional night patrol in No Man's Land. For the làtter volunteers were always called for, and the Americans were in every party.

Their active spirits found it even harder to bear than did their comrades. In December Thaw and two others managed to transfer to the aviation, declaring that they had pilot's certificates. After a few weeks as observer at Escadrille Deperdussin 6, Thaw managed to pass as pilot by the aid of Captain Degorge, commanding the Escadrille, and went off for his training on a Caudron at the aerodrome of Buc, taking his two friends with him. Thaw, who had flown a Curtiss, handled the Caudron without any difficulty, but the others had also said they were pilots and now it was up to them to prove it. One of them, Bert Hall, played the bluff out. He climbed alone into the machine that he was to try. It was the first time in his life that he had seen an aeroplane close to.

Off he went zig-zagging like a drunken duck, actually left the ground, but crashed headlong into the wall of a hangar. The machine was in pieces, but they picked him up unhurt to hear their verdict on his qualifications as a pilot. Then he began his training at the beginning.

Early in 1915 another American declared at the Avord school that he was a pilot and that he had even flown for long distances in Massachusetts. He was so vehement that they gave him a machine. He went off like a rocking horse, rose to 1500 feet, and from there dived headlong with motor full on. He never tried to flatten out and the machine crashed into fragments on the ground. It was literally reduced to match wood, but the pilot was picked up with nothing worse than a fractured knee. Extraordinary luck! . . . His name was Hardouin and he too had never been in a plane before.

In March, 1915, Thaw had passed all his tests and was sent at once to an Escadrille that was being formed at Nancy—the C. 42.

There he immediately distinguished himself in artillery observation and scouting. Once with his mechanic he tried to fight a Boche plane, his passenger having no other arm but a Winchester carbine. Thus equipped they cruised for hours over the lines, but the machine was too slow for them to overtake enemy planes, at that time few in number, but rather more numerous than our own.

In July, 1915, Thaw got a double motor Caudron G. 4, a much more powerful machine which could carry a mitrailleuse firing from in front. Then he was perfectly happy. But he wasn't yet able to bring down a Boche as his mitrailleuse used constantly to jam. Nevertheless he used to fly perseveringly for hours, indifferent to the cold.

At this time Escadrille 42, of which I had

just taken command, was at Lunéville. It used to go off and bombard the station of Metz, called "les Sablons." The Boches used to let us accomplish our job without interruption. Their Albatros would rise from the aerodrome of Frascati but fly low to protect the Zeppelin hangars without daring to get far away from the antiaircraft guns that protected them.

As Autumn passed into Winter the Escadrille was employed in "spotting" for our artillery against the big gun which the Boches had installed at Hampont to fire on Nancy. We managed to photograph this gun; then the bad weather of Winter brought a comparative truce.

The originator of the Escadrille was Norman Prince. He had passed a good deal of his life in France as his family lived at Pau, where his father was Master of the celebrated *pack* of foxhounds. In October, 1914, Prince had come forward to volunteer for the French army, but had only been able to get himself accepted in the Spring of '15. As he too was already a pilot he was able to continue his training in our schools. Then he passed into a bombing squadron which distinguished itself in Lorraine and

Artois. With a Voisin machine, fitted with an inch and a half gun, Prince was one of the first to devote himself to observation balloon chasing.

Bert Hall and Bach had been sent to the school at Pau. At the beginning they weren't very lucky in their training; indeed they smashed several machines. This fact, especially after their previous assertions that they knew how to fly, brought down on them the attention of the authorities, who began to ask if they weren't really spies trying to ruin our material and interfere with the training of pilots. Naturally there was no result to an enquiry on the subject, and after a short time they both became so competent as to be passed into a fighting squadron at the front. They flew Morane "parasols" whose great speed—for those days—of 70 miles an hour, made them first choice for fighting and long distance scouting.

One day Bach went off on a special mission, the dangerous job of putting down behind the enemy's lines a customs officer with a cage of carrier pigeons. He had already accomplished several of these missions successfully, which wasn't easy, for the Boches had a nasty habit of spotting the ground where an airman was likely to land and upsetting his machine by means of hidden wires. Both pilot and passenger thus captured were invariably shot without trial.

When one realizes the ordinary difficulty of starting an aeroplane at that time when the motor was nearly always tricky, to say nothing of the risks of capture, one can realize what courage was needed by the men employed in this work.

Bach landed all right, but broke his propellor in a ditch just as he was getting away. The Boches ran up and captured him. Luckily his passenger had escaped with his civilian clothes and his carrier pigeons. But the Boches tried Bach before two court-martials although they hadn't the slightest proof against him. He conducted his own defense with the greatest skill and managed to escape the firing squad.

Newcomers in the aviation, Cowdin, Chapman, Kiffin Rockwell and MacConnell, spent the last part of the year 1915 in completing their training as pilots at Avord and Pau. Prince, Cowdin, and Thaw went to spend Christmas, 1915, in the United States, where, as one might expect, they received the warmest of welcomes.

Norman Prince.

Kiffin Rockwell.

Funeral of Adjutant Prince.

Guynemer.

But they didn't waste their time and as result of their example and the publicity given to their exploits they found many eager to imitate them. The press took them up strongly and from this time public opinion in the United States began to regard the American pilots with pride as the nucleus of an American army in France. The pro-German newspapers loudly demanded their arrest, or at least that they should be forbidden to return to France. But the United States Government shut its eyes and they all came back to their post at the appointed time.

January, 1916, they reached Paris. During the journey back they had often discussed the question of forming an American Escadrille, composed solely of American volunteers.

Doubtless they were hardly numerous enough yet at the front, but besides the Foreign Legion, there was another source which supplied American pilots to our aviation schools. I refer to the Ambulance Corps. A plane moved faster than their Fords laden with wounded; it would be more sport, and they also felt that they could thus serve France's cause more directly.

An American Committee had been formed to

aid, encourage and recruit these pilots, and the first thing our young friends did on their return from America was to lay the project before it. The Committee at once espoused the idea of uniting all the American pilots in a single Escadrille.

At the head of this Committee were a distinguished French diplomat, Monsieur de Sillac, and Dr. Gros, the American surgeon of the Automobile Ambulance Section of the Field Service. One can never thank them enough for what they did, and we must also mention the valuable assistance which Mr. and Mrs. Vanderbilt gave to all the pilots who volunteered through this Committee. Soldiers in the French Army received one cent a day, no more. Our Americans found it insufficient but thanks to these benefactors they were able to live comfortably.

At the time when Prince, Cowdin and Thaw came back from America I happened to be on leave in Paris, having left my Escadrille in Nancy. I met them in the Rue Royale.

I was delighted with the idea, and after having discussed at considerable length with them how we should best set about it I accompanied them on their round of visits from office to office. We were helped by an Italian journalist Mr. Boggiano, who had just come back from America, and who knew some of our French public men. He introduced us to M. Pichon, manager Director of the *Petit Journal*, who is now Foreign Minister, and who promised to do his best for us.

The following day we went to see the Air Minister, René Besnard, who also said he would help us. The keenest supporter of the plan was Norman Prince, who declined to recognize difficulties. I had to calm him down or he'd have sent an ultimatum then and there to all the French authorities.

The Air Minister decided to permit the creation of this Escadrille in principle. While waiting for its actual formation Prince, Cowdin, and Thaw received permission to train on fighting planes. I went back to Nancy, which, however, I left shortly afterwards on a hurried summons to Verdun, where the Germans had just launched their great attack. Shortly after my arrival Thaw and Cowdin, whose training was finished, telephoned me from Paris saying how eager they were to begin work, and I managed to get them attached to a neighbouring battle squadron.

The officer in charge of aviation at General Headquarters, Major Barès, a man who took a big and farsighted view of things, was won over to the idea of an American Escadrille as soon as I spoke to him of it. He was able to appoint pilots on the front, and the Minister furnished mechanics and material at the beginning of April.

The battle of Verdun had then been raging for a month and a half, which made it difficult to move pilots about and consequently delayed the formation of the Escadrille.

How delighted I was when finally I received the order giving me the command of the American Escadrille—as we called it in those days. As my second I had obtained the appointment of my faithful friend Lt. de Laage de Meux, whose merits I had learned to appreciate while commanding a group of battle plane pilots in the Verdun sector.

I went off post-haste to Lyons to get the ten tractors, the four camions, the two light auto-

mobiles and the eighty men, mechanics, drivers,
cooks, secretaries, quartermasters, etc., which
form an escadrille. From Lyons I sent the material and personnel in a special train to Luxeuil
(Upper Saone) where the Escadrille was to be
formed. All the pilots ready received their orders to join up there immediately, the 18th of
April, 1916. The Quartermaster-Sergeant, a
fine fellow named Deville, sharpened his pencils
and opened his account book. The American
Escadrille N° 124 had come into being.

CHAPTER II

Luxeuil—Captain Happe—Alsace—First flights—First Successes

On the 20th of April, Chapman, Kiffin Rockwell, Norman Prince and MacConnell were the first to arrive. Thaw and Elliot Cowdin, whose work kept them on the Verdun front, only came a few days later, as did Bert Hall.

I went to introduce my pilots to Captain Happe, who commanded the Luxeuil bombing group.

Captain Happe—in the aviation we called him the "Red Pirate"—was famous for his mad recklessness, which was only equalled by his luck. He had been four times with his mechanic to bomb the Zeppelin factory at Friedrichshafen. He had turned his mitrailleuse on a train sixty miles behind the Boche lines and had made so many victims that the enemy put a price of 25,000 marks upon his head. He was worth more.

He always played the "lone wolf" game, fly-

ing an old 80 H. P. Maurice Farman nick-
named the "chicken-coop" because it had such
a network of wires in it. It had been built especially for him and was of pre-historic type—
good enough for family touring but quite un-
suitable for war. This machine only made forty
miles an hour, but its wing surface was so great
that it could carry a hundredweight of bombs and
lots of gasoline. The slowest enemy machine
could easily overtake it, play around it at will,
and shoot it up at pleasure. The mechanic was
armed with a Winchester carbine or a cavalry
musket, which he fired as best he could, sometimes even athwart the propellor. The "chicken-
coop" often came back with dozens of bullet
holes in its canvas framework, and even in the
propellor, but fortunately only the cage suffered,
the "chickens" never got a scratch.

Captain Happe once conceived the idea of
landing in Germany far behind the lines, near
some little railroad station, and carrying off the
station-master as prisoner in his plane so as to
get information from him. Luckily his superiors
formally forbade him to attempt this exploit for
fear that he would never come back.

To enable him to work on a bigger scale a
bombing group of four escadrilles had been
given him formed of the same type of machines
as his own. But the luck which had favoured
him did not hold for his subordinates, although
they were all remarkably skilled and courageous
pilots, who had begged to serve in his group well
knowing the dangers that awaited them. His
second in command, Lt. Almonacid, an Argen-
tine pilot as brave as he was skilful, took part
in all their expeditions. To reduce losses he
had wisely suggested that they should fly by
night—then a novelty—until they should receive
better machines.

When I entered Happe's office to introduce the
pilots of my escadrille we found him writing the
addresses on eight little boxes, sealed with seal-
ing-wax, which were in a row on his table. I
had known him a long time and after having
presented my pilots by name I asked what he was
doing. He replied: "These boxes contain the
eight war crosses which I am sending to the fam-
ilies of the eight pilots who were brought down
by the Boches the last time we bombed Habs-

heim!!!" As an introductory remark that
wasn't very encouraging. True, some Boches
had been brought down also. One airman, Captain X——, seeing his machine. had caught fire,
hurled himself upon the enemy who thought himself already victorious, and they fell to death together. Marinkowitch brought another down
point blank with his Bréguet gun. However,
the losses were heavy, and it was the intention of
our Chiefs that our Escadrille, when fully organized, should form a protection for Captain
Happe's group, no light task as you will understand. So the Captain greeted us as saviours
and exclaimed: "Hurry up and get ready as
quick as you can so that we can work together."
We all wanted the same thing though we knew
what the work would be and how heavy our re-
sponsibility. In the name of my pilots I promised him to be a good watch-dog for his flock.

For we were a real fighting escadrille, to our
very great delight. We were to fly the baby-
Nieuport, a machine which had made its appearance four months before, "the machine of
Aces and the Ace of machines" as we called it,

the fastest and handiest with its 16 square yards of surface, 80 H. P. Rhône rotary motor and speed of 95 miles an hour. For that period it was a tremendous advance. The Nieuport had won its spurs at Verdun, where it clearly outclassed the Fokker. It was our only fighting plane and in the French army one was thought immensely fortunate to fly it. When you flew a "Baby," so-called on account of its small dimensions, you were stamped at once as a great pilot and the crowd of other pilots envied you bitterly. You were no longer a taxi-chauffeur, whose part is to take out an observer who does all the really useful work, but the honoured driver of the fastest racing machine whose record-breaking speed and daring turns the press celebrated.

To fly a fighting machine meant the hope of becoming a past master in flight. All the most wonderful acrobatic tricks might be yours. Navarre had just invented aerial acrobatics with the spin, the renversement, the barrel [1] and had

[1] The spin is a rapid and jerky gyration of the machine round an axis generally vertical. When one doesn't expect it the impression is very disagreeable. The machine is entirely out of control. If one doesn't get out of the spin a crash is inevitable.

One gets into a spin as a result of a loss of speed. The machine brought to perfection the loop—words whose magic novelty had a glamour of their own. Only the Nieuports enabled us to accomplish these movements with full security and to approach our Boche with a disconcerting renversement or get away from him in the same way, manœuvres which now form the A B C of fighting tactics, but were only just beginning to be perfected at that period.

As armament we had a Lewis gun fixed on the upper plane and firing over the propellor (see photograph). This system had been discovered

falls and if the controls, instead of being kept well in neutral, are in an unsymmetrical position the spin begins.

To get out of the spin one should put the rudder to neutral if it is not there already, then push forward the joy stick and as soon as the spin breaks pull it back, bringing the plane to a level keel. Thus the spin is checked immediately and I cannot express the delight of a novice at feeling that once more he is handling a living machine which obeys him and not a dead thing over which he has no control.

How many pilots have been killed in the early days of aviation because they did not know how to stop a spin.

The barrel is a complete rotation of the machine around its horizontal axis. After the rotation one finds oneself in the same position and direction as before, simply a little further on in the same line of flight.

The renversement is more or less a half barrel followed by a loss of speed. You are then in a direction opposite the former one. It is thus a very rapid change of direction, which is very much used in fighting.

by our last hero Pégoud, with whom I had often flown over this same country of Alsace the preceding year, and whom I had gradually seen put his wonderful idea into practice.

This system enabled one to take position under an opponent's tail, to fire on him without his being able to see you, but it had certain drawbacks, due to the weapon, which I shall relate. To begin with, the drums of the machine gun only held 27 cartridges each. The Fokkers, however, had already adopted the system of the mitrailleuse firing through the screw by an arrangement of synchronization. Moreover our Lewis gun used to jam in 75 per 100 of our attacks owing to the effect of vibration, and many a Boche owed his life to that. So if we compared the Nieuport and the Fokker at that time, the former was superior as a machine in speed, handiness, climbing power and strength, but the Fokker had better armament. Taking them together the Nieuport was nevertheless regarded as far superior on account of its power of manœuvring and the confidence which it gave to pilots. So that it was no small honour that had been done us in supplying us with machines that were then the favourites of all the Air kings of those days.

At the beginning of the war fighting aviation didn't exist, and the first machines to be armed were Voisins with a "pusher" propellor, which were fitted with a Hotchkiss, according to the plans of Captain Mailfert. These machines were masters of the air until the end of 1914. With one of them Frantz had been the first French pilot to bring down a Boche in an air battle near Rheims. The Morane "Parasol" with a passenger armed with a carbine had held sway in 1915, and an army was considered to be protected as far as the air was concerned when one machine patrolled twenty-five or thirty miles of front. That was the best that could be done owing to the lack of machines.

In 1915 little single-seater fighting planes had begun to make their appearance. Then that great pilot Garros had had the idea of armourplating the propellor of a small Morane so that he could fire his machine gun athwart the whirling blade without fear of its being splintered by a bullet. Should any touch the propellor the armour deflected them and prevented damage.

After several successes Garros had been captured in Flanders.[1]   The Germans had copied his machine and developed from it the Fokker.   Gilbert had gone on working where Garros had left off, and Pégoud had made further improvements on the Nieuport.   He had been the first to fix a Lewis gun on the upper plane firing above the propellor.   In 1915 I had worked with both these heroes, who had lost their lives, Pégoud in battle against a great armoured plane, and Gilbert by accident, and I had seen their efforts gradually crowned with success.   I remember even one day while patrolling in a G-4 over the Vosges towards Kahler-Wasen my mitrailleur, a young observer, had poured a hail of bullets at Pégoud's Nieuport thinking that he was a Boche.   Up to then we had never seen biplanes like his with the canvas covered tail.   I spotted the French colours and by a sudden renversement put it out of my gunner's power to continue his fell design; but that evening by way of fine and excuse to Pégoud, and also to celebrate Gilbert's victory

---

[1] As all the world knows he succeeded in escaping after many abortive attempts, only to be killed in aerial combat a few weeks before the armistice. His death was mourned by the whole country.

over a big German biplane brought down at Thann, we had to buy a case of good champagne and some bottles of old Alsace wine.

Up to 1916 all fighting was done singly and patrol work was rare, but at Verdun, at the beginning of '16, the Boches had started using patrols successfully. Indeed at first they had caused much perturbation in the ranks of our Farmans, good observation machines, but too slow and too unhandy for fighting. So, to retaliate, we had had to follow suit and I had determined to spare no pains in training my pilots to fly in good formation.

All we had to do was to wait for our machines which were coming from Paris by road on automobile tractors. It was a fortnight before we got them, for Verdun, where France's destiny was at stake, consumed nearly all the available output.

We established ourselves on the fine aerodrome of Luxeuil, the biggest and most beautiful in France; it is over two miles long, entirely flat, surrounded by a circuit of high hills, the last outposts of the Vosges mountains.

The French used one end of it; at the other

were grouped British airmen of the Royal Navy, Canadians, Australians, or South Africans, of whom we shall have occasion to speak later. I found quarters for my pilots in the charming little town of Luxeuil Baths, a peaceful oasis, forty miles behind the lines, which had almost never had any troops stationed there and was delighted to welcome aviators. I have often seen friends who had spent some time at Luxeuil after us. They all told me "after your escadrille had gone away it was impossible to beat the good record that your Americans had left behind in the hearts of everyone. All were sorry to lose them."

As its name shows, Luxeuil was a thermal watering place, an old town with Renaissance houses, curiously carved. In one of the finest Francis I once spent the night, and the house still bore his name. Lt. de Laage lived there while I established myself at Baths' Hotel.

In the morning we all used to go down to the bath house and bathe in the pink granite pools where the elegant belles of Louis XV's reign had been wont to repair the weariness of court life. Most of our pilots stayed at the Ho-

Lt. De Laage de Meux.

Lufbery.

Presentation of flag to Lafayette Escadrille.

Presentation of flag to Lafayette Escadrille.

tel of the Golden Apple, a really good old French inn, where we used all to meet for meals. What a fine place it was! The regular type of the inns of Old France, whose proprietors followed one another from father to son in unbroken line for centuries, where every visitor was treated as one of the family. The cooking was famous, delicious trout from a neighbouring stream, fat chickens, game, hares, wild-fowl, and good dishes carefully cooked and washed down with generous Burgundy, whose aroma alone was enough to make your head swim. And withal extraordinarily cheap, "Board and Lodging 4 francs a day." The proprietors weren't so much in business to make money as to keep up the good name of their house. Before the war that wasn't as uncommon in France as one might think. It has changed a good deal since, but that's on account of the war, as everyone says.

Imagine how welcome was the restful calm of Luxeuil after the hell of Verdun, where nerves had been taut to the breaking point and one had to fight with every ounce of one's strength not to win, but simply to hold on; where against the

Boche who had carefully prepared his attack
we had had to put up a defence on the spur of
the moment and struggle desperately against ten
times our number of assailants.

In our light automobiles we used to go into
Alsace and visit aerodromes where I had already
been, some of them located only eight miles behind the lines, which would be later ports of call
for us. Between Luxeuil and the line these
aerodromes of Belfort, Fontaine, and Romagny
were the only available refuges. In an area of
more than 35 miles which we crossed through the
gap of Belfort or across the Vosges, there were
no other landing fields, so that these needed
to be thoroughly familiar to our pilots, especially
as they were rather hard to recognize at first.

We had a good deal of trouble from Switzerland, which used to make a lot of fuss when our
planes flew over its territory. Some of the Americans who were not very familiar with map-
reading used to be misled by the fact that there
is no natural line of demarcation between the
two countries. So I had to teach them to recognize the most distinctive features of the land-
scape. In our trips along the frontier we would

pass the time of day with the officer of the Swiss guard post at Rechesy, the frontier village, and stuff our machine full of cigars whose flavour was doubly good because they were contraband. In the course of these trips we used to examine carefully the dimensions of the various aerodromes we visited as well as the natural obstacles around them. The roads over which we passed were fringed with cherry trees in blossom and a hearty lunch in some Alsatian inn at Dannemarie or elsewhere would break our journey. The greeting of mine host was as welcome as his good cheer, washed down with Alsace's wine and a drop of its famous Kirsch at the end. We used to come back by the Valley of Thann or by Belfort, Giromagny and the Ballon of Alsace. My pilots were amazed by the beauty of the country, with its torrents roaring in waterfalls over the cliffs on the steep pineclad slopes of the mountains. These pines of Alsace, symbolic trees, how majestically their great trunks towered up to Heaven! In voyages like these our American comrades learned to understand some of the love that we Frenchmen bear our country.

It was a short trip down the Valley of Thann and then our car would climb the pass of Bussang. After the tunnel at its summit we would go down the French side in a series of giddy zig-zags, and there the valley of the Moselle opened before us. Everywhere on our trips we used to make note of the few possible places for landing in case of accident, some of them just square patches of field less than fifty yards each way. It was enough to make you shudder to look at them—and all around them great trees, hills, ravines and innumerable electric power lines, especially in the valley of Thann which was filled with busy factories. Let us bear in mind these electric power lines for later they were to cost the life of one of our comrades.

Then we would get back home to Luxeuil by the fine straight road from Faucogney, after having climbed again the pass of La Fourche.

It was a pleasant journey through the perfumed air, but we could not help thinking of our French comrades in their truceless struggle before Verdun. Our forced inactivity worried us. I sent telegram after telegram to hurry the arrival of the Nieuports, with the result that at

last to our immense joy they reached us on the
first of May. Six baby Nieuports, three with
110 H.P. Rhône and three with 80 H.P. Rhône.
Specialist workmen from the Nieuport firm
hastened to assemble our machines and we set our
mechanics to work, especially in fixing the machine guns. The planes had come bare; we had
to put on the armament ourselves. Once assembled we tried them immediately, although few
of us had ever flown a Nieuport; everything went
off all right.

The terrible storm of the 10th of May, 1916,
will never be forgotten by those who experienced
it, so sudden and so furious was the wind. On
the French front all the "sausages" were torn
from their moorings and despite their parachutes
a dozen observers were killed by being dragged
along the soil.

The canvas hangars, unsheltered from the
wind, were upset like mere houses of cards. Any
machines that were out in the field were swept
away like straws, borne hundreds of yards on
the tempest, and battered to pieces as they fell.

It had been a fine afternoon and Kiffin Rockwell was trying his machine over the aerodrome.

There was a dark line across the horizon towards the south-west, but at Luxeuil the sun was shining and the air calm. Suddenly this line seemed to rush upon him in a few moments at terrific speed. It was a cloud of dust raised by the cyclone. The sun was hidden immediately, but from the ground we could witness Rockwell's struggle with the tempest. His Nieuport was thrown up and down like a dead leaf, but the pilot kept his head. He started descending head straight to the wind, with his motor full on and joystick right forward. The force of the wind was so great that he didn't go forward at all, but came down gradually. Our mechanics gauged the spot where this new fangled helicopter was going to land. They ran to meet it. Rockwell landed right in their midst and immediately a score of vigorous hands gripped his fragile machine by the wheels, the wings, the supports or the fuselage—anywhere, so as to prevent it being whirled away. Rockwell got out safe and sound and his machine was uninjured. It was a splendid piece of work.

In those days there was shortage of machines owing to the limited production, and a pilot who broke his plane was likely to remain some time without another or be put back on to a slower and easier machine like the old Farman.

To have had a glimpse of the life of a modern Knight of the Air and then to go back down the scale to become a cabby driving a weary old jade, what a dreadful rise and fall!

Our mechanics worked madly. I busied myself in getting the last accessories needed, and as for our pilots they never left their machines. Our leisurely walks at twilight, along the narrow lanes scented with honeysuckle, were a thing of the past. From early dawn everyone dashed to the aerodrome and helped his mechanic.

Moreover, if we needed any stimulus we'd have got it from the fact that several Boches had passed over the ground on scouting expeditions at a great height. They had doubtless been warned by their espionage service, which benefited by the proximity of Switzerland, of the work which was being done at the Luxeuil aerodrome, and had come to verify their information. We foresaw that they would not be long in coming to bomb us, and it maddened us to be unable to rise and attack them.

At last all our machines were ready. As we had never made patrols together we planned out our first trip with great care. Each of us had marked his plane with special emblems, so as to be clearly visible in the air and be recognized by his leaders and fellow-airmen. Big MacConnell had adopted a cabalistic sign of a huge footprint painted white.

The machines were drawn up long before the appointed hour. The route had been studied out, the formation decided, the point of rendezvous settled beforehand, and our mission fully understood. It was to cruise along from a point three miles from the Swiss frontier up to Mulhouse at an altitude of ten thousand feet. Everything then was ready and we left on a fine morning flying in a wild-duck wedge, Rockwell at the head. I was last of one file to keep an eye on my colts, and on the other side Thaw as a skilled pilot to protect that file. We were over Belfort twenty minutes later.

Below us Vauban's old forts seemed to slumber peacefully. Despite its huge size we couldn't distinguish the Lion hewn out by the sculptor Bartholdi from the living rock of the fortress

Our mascots.   The dog Fram.

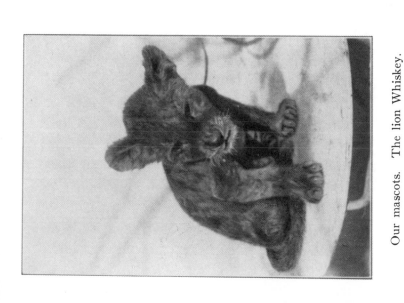

Our mascots.   The lion Whiskey.

The Escadrille after Prince's death, Lufbery absent.

to commemorate its heroic resistance in the war
of 1870.

Far, far away to westward, far across the
ocean, at the entry of America's greatest port,
another statue of the same sculptor held aloft
its symbolic torch. Which of us would have
thought that two years later armed men in mil-
lions would be leaving that great port to come
to France's aid and that the streets of that little
old French town would be thronged with khaki
uniforms side by side with horizon blue?

Our motors were soaring away without a miss.
Soon we had passed the modern fort of Roppe
and the hangars of Fontaine came into sight.
Two French "sausages" and two Boches were
swaying at the end of their frail moorings. Between them the trenches, the line. It was our
first thrill—we were now over enemy soil.

Our patrol had got a little scattered, but one
couldn't expect perfection on the first time out.
One pilot indeed was getting alarmingly far from
the rest of us; it was MacConnell who had missed
his way. Dazzled by the sun, he no longer saw
the other planes and was making off danger-
ously near Switzerland. Alas poor neutrality!

Another diplomatic incident in perspective. I opened up my 110 H.P. and managed to overtake MacConnell and bring him back by signs into line.

We had lost sight of the others, but black shell-bursts north-east of us showed where they must be. We dived towards the black smoke blobs and soon after joined the patrol circling round a little south-west of Mulhouse just above the forest of Nonnenbruch and the anti-aircraft batteries hidden there.

The latter were firing for all they were worth. "Who are these lunatics who are staying right over our heads instead of trying to get into a quieter sector?" the Boche artillerymen must have thought.

In fact it needed plenty of nerve to remain in the midst of this furnace. Right and left, above, below, shellbursts surrounded us and my pilots actually seemed to find it amusing. The novices, Chapman, MacConnell and Rockwell, deliberately amused themselves by diving at the little smoke clouds. . . . Meanwhile the strident explosions of the shells continued. Perhaps what nailed them to the spot was the beauty of the scenery. From the air much scenery appears monotonous, everything looks flat and uniform, but the valley of the Rhine is an exception. In the midst of the plain a long silver ribbon, the Rhine, and all around the mountain crests encircle the low ground like a great amphitheatre. On the east it is the Vosges, to the south-west the Jura and the massive Mont Blanc in all its dazzling majesty. On the south the Swiss Alps, the Oberland and the proud peak of the Jungfrau; then, to end the circle, the Swabian Jura and the Black Forest. What a wonderful picture it was!

I didn't find it sufficient, however, to keep my pilots right above several anti-aircraft batteries. What really made them stay was the absence of Boches. They thought that the German aviators would have rushed up at the sight of the shellbursts that revealed our presence, just as they themselves would have done in similar circumstances. As a further hint to the enemy Rockwell dived right down over the Habsheim aerodrome and there performed an aerial fandango to bring the Boches out. But either they refused to be drawn or they were already far away; the guns alone continued their unpleasant chorus.

We followed Rockwell who as leader of the patrol we wouldn't have abandoned at any price. At last he decided to leave this hell, where evidently there were no Boche planes to be found, as their gunners fired so steadily, and led us off southwards to a calmer spot.

It was a long way home, and we had only just enough gas to get back to our ground if we didn't want to land "in the cabbages" as we French say. In this case the "cabbages" were pine trees on the flank of precipitous mountains, and the lowest trees in sight were oaks on the jagged foot hills.

We went back straight by the Valley of Massevaux. Below us glittered the Lake of Sewen, which had been formed by a dam inaugurated some years before with great ceremony by the Kaiser. On that day the old Alsatian town of Massevaux had shuttered its windows like a city of the dead. It had died indeed in '71 with the Treaty of Frankfort, but the entry of our troops had brought it back to life again. Then came the Ballon of Alsace and its bald summit, the

Ballon of Servance with its fort, and thence twenty-five miles away we perceived the hangars of Luxeuil.

Good workmanlike landing. Altogether a promising first expedition,—only next time we hoped for some Boches.

Our mechanics were eagerly awaiting us. Directly we landed they ran up and helped us to get back to our hangars. Minor imperfections in our machines were pointed out to them and after having filled up with gas they started working on them, as well as on the machine-guns whose trials had been rather unsatisfactory. I have said that we had Lewis guns, mounted on the upper plane. The trigger was actuated by a Bowden wire and to put a new drum in—for the 27 cartridges were soon shot away—you had to swing the weapon down by pulling a lever (see photo) and the wind brought it sharply backwards at the risk of cracking your skull if you didn't keep your head well down. It was far from an easy job to substitute a full drum for an empty one with your fingers frozen and hampered by thick gloves, and one needed quite a lot of practice to do it properly, especially as one had to use one hand for piloting the ship for fear of getting into a spin.

Only a practised pilot could repair a machine-gun jam in the air, so that in a fight there was always the danger of being disarmed against an adversary who could fire five hundred cartridges at a clip. We had not had time to get all the practice needed for this sort of work, but the experience of our first trip showed that it was necessary, so I prevented my pilots from going out immediately back to the lines and set them all to this job. They continued their machine gun training that afternoon over the aerodrome and found themselves fortunate when the wind didn't carry away the drum before it had been fixed in place. In that case it was good-bye to the drum, and one could only hope it didn't land on the head of anyone down below. In actual fighting this mishap would have been serious, for your adversary with his superior weapon had a good chance of bringing you down while you were busy trying to fix up your own.

So we had good reason to work hard at this task and gradually we got satisfactory results with the help of a whole series of little improvements due to the ingenuity of our mechanics.

Always on leaving the aerodrome we hurried famished to the hotel and there was no lack of conversation at meals. In the morning we talked French, English at night. It was forbidden to make a mistake of a single word under pain of ten cents to the pool. The result was that some hard-headed citizens endeavoured to maintain unbroken silence but they couldn't stand the kidding of their friends which would go on until they simply had to answer; then they'd burst out into a weird Franco-American jargon that would have made the fortune of a clown in the circus.

But our pleasant repose began to be singularly troubled. The Boche, who had been growing more and more uneasy over the development of Luxeuil, came one night on a bombarding expedition, and four of our devoted mechanics were blown to bits. The German machine had flown very high, then cut out its engine, and planed down unheard to plant its bombs with certainty on our slumbering crew.

Against attacks like these we were powerless; night fighting is a myth regarding which the civilian population has been hoodwinked too long. Against night raiders there is nothing really of avail save an extraordinarily well-organized artillery defence from the ground. It was only towards the end of the war that one began to have perfected systems of guns firing at an invisible objective according to data furnished by range finding from sound. Results were limited enough even then, but before this discovery of calculating an aeroplane's position by the sound of its motors there was nothing but a few searchlights, whose value was entirely illusory and which often served rather to enable the bombing plane to locate its objectives.

Nevertheless, as it was light very early and the German machines used to come over but a short time before dawn we used to bring out our planes in the night to start as best we could in the darkness directly we heard the ominous buzz of their motor, so as to go and await them over the Vosges at daybreak on their way back. It was pretty dangerous, for motor trouble by night over this mountainous and thickly wooded country with our swift machines would have meant certain death.

At this sort of game Thaw was desperate and

Escadrille 42 leaves Luneville to bomb the station of Metz.

Lt. Thaw leaves the ground.

Tragic photograph—the four first arrivals at the Escadrille.

Mac Connell   Rockwell   Prince   Chapman   (All were killed.)

persevering, but he never had the luck to bring down an enemy, although sometimes he managed to get in touch with them. Perhaps, like the rest of us, he wasn't sufficiently expert in the awkward work of firing from a single-seater, whose full difficulty we none of us yet realized.

Rockwell was the first to have the good fortune to bring down a Boche plane.

He was cruising one fine morning—it was the 18th of May—between Mulhouse and the Hartmannsweilerkopf, when he perceived a big German biplane with its black crosses trying to cross over our line. It was an L.V.G. He dived and fired a burst of five or six cartridges at it which brought it down in the enemy's lines. You may imagine how we fêted our Escadrille's first victory. Rockwell's brother sent us from Paris a bottle of whiskey eighty years old, a real treat for a connoisseur. We at once decided that only pilots who brought down Boches could drink a glass for each victory. A certain Lufbery was destined to drink half the bottle all by himself.

The following day, May 19th, we received orders to make for the region of Verdun, where the struggle was still very fierce, and to locate ourselves at Béhonne near Bar-le-Duc. We were delighted, for there were lots of Boche planes at Verdun and we were certain of good sport. Our pilots were now getting into form and we looked forward confidently to the future. We hoped to avenge the great French fliers of that epoch, who had just been put out of action, Navarre and Chaput, who had been wounded, and Boillot, the famous racing automobile champion before the war, who had been killed.

In the night of the 19th to the 20th all our automobile tractors were drawn up at the edge of the field, loaded and ready to start, when an enemy bombing plane by a lucky shot—lucky for him but the reverse for us—dropped an explosive charge right in the middle of them. The gasoline in the tanks caught fire and four of our wagons were completely destroyed. The others were only saved by the devotion of some mechanics, who started them off despite the machine gun fire of the Boche, who came down and scattered bullets over the blaze. However, nobody was wounded.

Trenches in Alsace; Oberer, Ochsene, Eldhop.
It will be noticed that the trenches are intact as the sector was quiet.

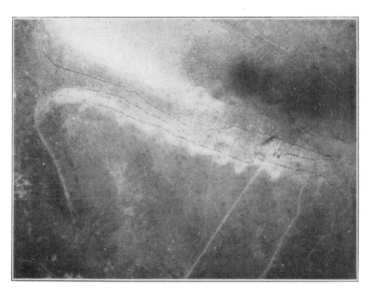

Trenches at Les Eparges.   Notice the great mine craters.

Crater caused by the explosion of a bomb dropped by a German plane on the field of Luxeuil.

CHAPTER III

Verdun—A Great Battle at its height—Chapman—The
Escadrille distinguishes itself

At Luxeuil we had had a narrow escape at the
last minute. Now "Verdun! Verdun!" was the
general cry and at dawn I gave the signal for
departure. Captain Happe lent us extra camions
for our mechanics to replace those we had lost.
For us pilots it was only too easy to travel as the
crow flies; I gave orders to follow the lines and
land at Lunéville to fill up with gas. What a
delightful trip it was over the blue Vosges, with
here and there mist, making a light veil at the
bottom of the valleys. The lakes of Gerardmer
and Longemer glittered in the sunlight like splendid emeralds.

At Lunéville the aerodrome is small and almost enclosed in the town. From up above you
wonder how you are going to land on this tiny
pocket handkerchief. However our landing was
accomplished all right. The Escadrille at Luné-

ville N⁰ 48 kept us for lunch. During the meal two Boches came over the town. Thaw and Chapman dashed off to the ground and chased them swiftly home again. Chapman gave me a moment of great anxiety in diving so sharply after them into the enemy's lines that we thought he had been brought down. In the afternoon we went on towards Bar-le-Duc. At Nancy, Hall left the patrol to make a little tour in the direction of Metz. It wasn't the time for a thing like that. However, he soon found that he was getting lost and decided to follow us again. At Béhonne, whose aerodrome, situated on a plateau, surrounded by deep ravines immediately north of Bar-le-Duc, is dreaded for its difficulties, our landing was accomplished without accident.

With his usual kindness, Major Fabiani, who I am sorry to say died shortly afterwards, placed at our disposal a comfortable villa right at the gates of the town, which had been abandoned by its owner. It soon became the rendezvous at lunch hour for all the French pilots passing through Bar-le-Duc. We kept open table and in a very short time had firmly established our reputation for hospitality.

Those of us who had not yet got machines received them immediately and those who were ready had no time to waste, for there was plenty of work to do. Our French comrades were overwhelmed by it. They had nevertheless begun to get the upper hand over the enemy aviation, but at the price of many sacrifices. Their task was a heavy one and it was up to us to help them. You can imagine that our boys wanted nothing better. The word "Verdun" had keyed them to the highest pitch. On the 22nd we began to work. There was a big counter-attack that day by the French, and the aviation had an important rôle to play in the thunderous concert. We were instructed to patrol at the height of a thousand feet in the region of Douaumont, where the artillery battle was chiefly concentrated.

On days of battle there were three stages for patrols (later there were as many as six); the low patrol at a thousand feet, middle at six thousand, and high at twelve thousand, all of them working over the battle zone. If you were twelve thousand feet up there might be heavy air-fighting going on near the ground without your knowing anything about it, and vice-versa. In the latter case it was quite impossible for you to take part even if you wanted to, because it took too long to get up to the required altitude. During our flight we could hear the roar of the very large shells and sometimes even see them in the form of a passing flash. In our pilot's slang we called them the big black rats, and there was no small danger of being involved in their trajectory. Sometimes an aeroplane literally burst into fragments, which meant that a big shell had hit it in full career.

In war, life, or rather death, is only a question of meeting on your own route with the trajectories of any kind of projectile. To escape, the only thing to do is not to be at the meeting point at the same moment.

It was really surprising that this accident didn't happen more often, especially in the case of the low patrols, which were the least sought after on account of this ever present risk.

The 25th at dawn Thaw, on a patrol with Rockwell, was lucky enough to bring down a Fokker. "No credit to me," he told us, "I just murdered him. He never saw me."

Immediately after their return we made a grand

scouting expedition over the lines along the whole
sector.   The Escadrille in full force was to take
the opportunity of sweeping the sky good and
clear.   What a trip that was!   I'll remember
it all my life.   Thaw and Rockwell had only
just time to fill up their tanks when I gave my
orders, which were that we should only attack
if I gave the signal by see-sawing my plane.   We
were to follow the lines; I knew the Boche, knew
that he had all his great aces, Boelke and the
rest of them, in the neighbourhood, and I wanted
to train my escadrille before trying to stack up
against them.   So, I was anxious not to lose the
fight almost before it began by attempting to
go too fast.   As a matter of fact it was the lack
of this sort of gradual training for battle practised on the battle-field itself, which later caused
the pilots of the American Expeditionary Force
to incur such cruel losses.   But to go back to our
trip.

We went off in the direction of Saint Mihiel.
The patrol formed up correctly over Les Eparges,
with its immense mine craters as big as volcanoes,
and we flew over the lines always followed by
the shells of anti-aircraft guns, which were so

numerous in this sector that even later we never saw them thicker anywhere else.

We turned northwards and immediately a strange sight met our eyes: a strip of ground several miles wide without a tree, without grass, brown and yellow in color, where the soil was pitted with shell-holes innumerable that touched each other, without roads, without houses, nothing—nothing, as if the very bowels of the earth had been torn open. It was the battlefield of Verdun. Fort Douaumont could still just be distinguished. Suddenly, in the distance eastwards, towards Etain, I perceived a dozen Boche two-seaters, flying low over their own lines, so low that they seemed like sheep grazing on the green meadows far from the cannon-ravaged zone.

They were too low, too numerous, and too far behind their own lines for us to attack on this first expedition, especially with pilots who had yet to get thoroughly acquainted with a redoubtable enemy. For when one goes down low over enemy territory one has always to remember the danger which may come from above, against which one is powerless.

Suddenly a pilot, I don't know who it was,

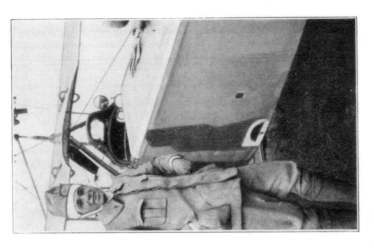

Paul Rockwell regarding the spot where his brother was brought down.   Hartmannsweilerkopf in background.

Chapman, though wounded, wants to renew the fight.

A Nieuport Vickers.

A fort at the West of Verdun.

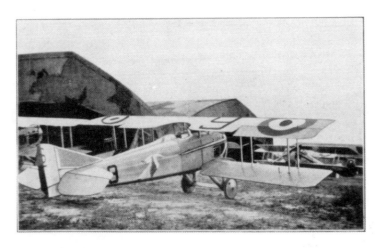

At cachy — a Spad of the Stork Escadrille.

An enemy plane burned the Stork's hangar.

Cachy Wood in the snow.

Dudley Hill.

whether de Laage or another, we were never able to find out, dived like a meteor straight towards the Boches. Without the least hesitation everyone followed, joysticks right forward at full speed. Everyone picked out his opponent, but the Boches were so startled to see this pack of devils falling upon them that they turned tail and ran for all they were worth. Then our machine guns came into play and the Boches replied.

Everyone of us was so busy that he lost sight of his comrades and watched only the enemy, who tried to meet us from in front and on the flank and above all were anxious not to let us catch them in the rear during their flight. They dived for home and we followed them. At least three enemy were seriously hit and landed one after the other. I saw two of our machines turn back towards our lines, also hit as we learned afterwards.

The Boches were much too low for us. We could see the soldiers firing at us in the street of Etain; it was time to make back for our lines. The retreat was carried out in good order; the Boche had been attacked too savagely to think of pursuing us, and by good fortune there were none of them up above. Nothing worse than the disagreeable boom of their guns followed us homewards. At last we saw the lines in the distance; then passed the enemy's "sausages," beyond them our own lines, and so back again into calm.

I was anxious to get back to our ground at Bar-le-Duc to reassemble my pilots. Were there any missing? I couldn't tell. We were too scattered. The journey back, despite my Nieuport's speed, seemed very long to me.

I landed. A big fellow, his face all covered with blood, was waiting for me. It was Kiffin Rockwell, who burst into a flood of abuse against Germany and her disloyal methods. In fact an explosive bullet had burst on his windshield and cut his upper lip. A slight wound, which only lent fuel to his ardour.

Everyone was now home save Thaw. Our uneasiness was growing, yet no one had seen a French machine come down as if it was out of control, but in the midst of such a mêlée one can never tell what is going on a few yards away.

In a fight like that two machines cross each other at hundred miles an hour, firing furiously,

and sometimes the fight is all over in the fraction
of a second.   If you just glance away for a moment the whole action may have happened without your noticing it.

We went to lunch in the town having arranged
that any news which might come should be telephoned to us.

Everyone had an incident of the fighting to
relate, and we hoped that Thaw had managed
to land in our lines.   Sure enough.   The telephone rang, I rushed to it, and after having
shouted "Hello" a dozen times, for there were
a number of intermediate posts, through which
communication had to pass, I learned that Thaw
had had an arm broken by a bullet, but that he
had managed to land nearly dead-beat on a
ground near the lines close to the fort of Ta-
vannes right on top of the Côtes de Meuse.   He
had been picked up by one of our Regiments
and taken to the hospital of Dieue.

That was almost good news, since he wasn't
killed, and at Verdun that was the most one could
hope for.   That afternoon I went to see him.
The roads were choked, for the Germans were
firing on the Meuse bridges.   Shells were burst-

ing in the water, raising splendid fountains. Fish floated belly upwards on the surface and our poilus, careless of the shell fire, picked them out with nets, delighted with the addition to their mess.   We found Thaw comfortably fixed up and well looked after.   They were going to put his arm in plaster and send him off two days later to the American hospital at Neuilly on the outskirts of Paris.   He told us that while he was engaged in a combat he received from the German machine-gunner a ball which had fractured his left elbow.   Despite the agony of the wound and the loss of blood he was able to keep control of his plane.

He had only one thought—to get back westwards.   Quite exhausted, he landed in the barbed wire without knowing where he was.   Then he saw blue uniforms.   He was saved.

On the 24th of May there came to the escadrille a pilot whom I was too busy to take much notice of the first day, but who rapidly attracted everyone's attention.   Simple, modest, silent and hardworking, always getting his plane ready himself—it was Lufbery.

Several other new pilots came to join us.   First

of all young Balsley, who had all the shyness and gentleness of a girl, but whose soul was that of a man, as he soon showed.   Then came Chouteau-Johnson, Rumsey and Dudley Hill; the latter was destined to stay with the escadrille to the end, comrade of good and evil days alike.   There came too Didier-Masson, an old pilot, who had already made his début in aerial warfare with Carranza's army in its rebellion against Huerta.   He then flew an old-fashioned Blériot.

The 17th of June—I remember it as if it was yesterday—we were patrolling on the right bank of the Meuse and were supposed to remain there, but Chapman saw that all the Boches were on the left bank and, like a tiger, dashed at a group of them.   What a lot of enemy planes there were on the left bank, a regular swarm.   With Balsley and de Laage we followed and freed him from the attack of a big camouflaged plane, a heavily armed three-seater, which despite its bitter resistance, was forced to dive for safety to Forges wood. We turned homewards satisfied, but Chapman didn't come right back to the Béhonne aerodrome. After having filled up with gas at Vadelaincourt he went off alone again.   He met a Boche ace, who handled his machine infernally well, as Chapman told us afterwards, accompanied by four others. Chapman stood up to him all right, but his plane was riddled with bullets, one of which slightly wounded him in the head (see photo) and he was forced to land at Froidos, the field of Escadrille 67, with a machine that was no longer air-worthy; several struts had been almost completely cut through. He had been fighting with Boelke, the famous German pilot, a clever oldstager, who, by the way, told the story of the fight in one of his letters. So keen was Chapman that my friend, Captain de Saint-Sauveur, commanding the 67th, had to give him positive orders not to attempt another flight with his injured "cuckoo." He wanted to go and have another shot at them and despite his wounds utterly declined to rest. He was so disappointed at being forced to part with his machine while it was being repaired that I had to give him another immediately.

On the 19th of June Balsley, while engaged with a Fokker north of Verdun, was surprised by another machine. Close by, I myself was busy with two others. Balsley received an explosive bullet in the thigh which caused appalling injuries, literally splitting the pelvis bone. His machine got into a spin. . . .

By sheer will-power—God knows how he managed it with such a wound—Balsley managed to recover control and land near Fort of Choiseul quite close to the first line, where our brave infantrymen, heedless of shellfire, picked him up and carried him to the shelter of a comfortless First Aid Post, established at the bottom of a squalid cellar. All the surgeon could do for him was to apply a temporary bandage.

Fortunately an automobile was in the neighbourhood, which had come for an officer who, while acting as observer in a "sausage," had been forced to jump out with his parachute. A German battery had cut the "Sausage's" cable and as the wind was blowing towards the enemy lines, the officer had chosen to leap for it rather than be taken prisoner. It was a lucky accident for Balsley, for he had received intestinal injuries which required an immediate operation. The automobile took him swiftly back to the hospital of Vadelaincourt, where he was admirably cared for by an Infirmière Major of the French Red Cross, Madame Dorville. The surgeon who operated didn't try to hide from us the gravity of the case. Balsley had to lie on his back for more than a year, but the care that he received snatched him from death; he gradually began to get better and our hopes revived.

On the 23rd of June Balsley sent us a telephone message that he would like some oranges, orange juice being the only nourishment allowed him, as his intestine was perforated in several places by splinters of the explosive bullet.

Immediately that good fellow Chapman offered to carry him some on his Nieuport. On the way, Chapman couldn't resist the temptation of attacking the foe who had brought Balsley down. Far off northwards numerous shell-bursts with white smoke, which proved they were French, for the German's were black, showed there was "game" in the air. He met a troop of five Fokkers, perhaps Boelke again, but joined battle without hesitating, only to be brought down in the enemy lines at Haumont near Samogneux.

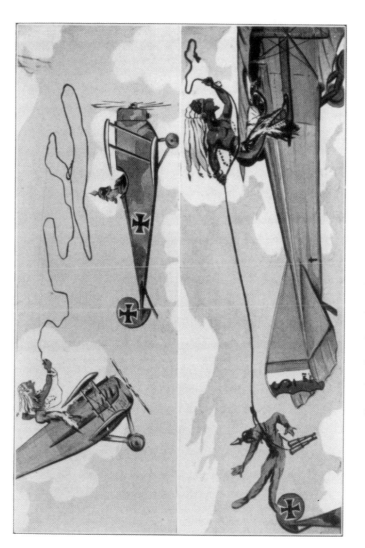

Imaginative drawings inspired by our emblem.

Lt. Féquant.   Thenault.   Thaw.   Lufbery.

In its fall his machine broke in the air. An observer on a Farman told us the story of the fight and with what gallant courage our comrade had battled. Glory to Chapman, that true hero! Men like him are the pride of a Nation, their names should ever be spoken with respect.

The American Escadrille was now beginning to attract attention and General Headquarters sent us a hail of decorations.

On July 4th, Independence Day, there was a big fête in Paris, and with some of my pilots I went to represent the Escadrille at the ceremony at Lafayette's tomb in Picpus cemetery. There the American Ambassador, the Honourable Mr. Sharp, made a speech whose form might appear diplomatic, but in every phrase of which was clearly revealed the affection of his country for our own.

At this time Nungesser came to stay with us for a few days and went to work with his usual dash, flying his Nieuport with its famous but ghoulish insignia the Death's Head and Cross Bones, and brought down an enemy plane.

My second in command, Lieutenant de Laage

de Meux, brought down a German on the 27th of July between Ornes and Bezonvaux. He was one of the most determined pilots in the Escadrille and yet he was a long time in getting his first victory, owing to a run of bad luck.

On the 31st of July we were having lunch when a telephone message informed us that Lufbery had brought down a Boche. He too had well earned success by his perseverance.

Once he had begun, he went on in the same vein bringing down two more near Fort Vaux and a fourth on the 8th of August near Douaumont in the Ravine of the Viper.

That was the tenth Boche brought down by the Escadrille. On the 16th of August Lufbery received the Military Medal and the War Cross with one palm. He was scoring successes faster than they could recompense him.

As I have already said the Germans had got together a strong force of aviation for this battle of Verdun. They profited by it to fly over and bombard Bar-le-Duc during July and August, causing serious damage each time.

The town was so near the St. Mihiel Gap, only

fifteen miles away, that the whole business was over and done with before we could rise to fight them. Moreover, they used generally to come while we were on patrol over the lines north of Verdun.

They came in groups of twenty or thirty and did a great deal of harm to the town. Once we had to rise and fight them while a hail of bombs were falling round us on the field with their horrible whistling as they fell—Ugh! . . . It's a most unpleasant position to be sitting out in the middle of an aerodrome in a machine whose motor is slow in starting while bombs are falling all around you. The mechanic twists away at the propellor in vain and when at last the motor does decide to fire it's a tremendous relief, for you know that at last you will be able to meet the enemy on fair terms. Until you start you keep thinking that each bomb, whose ominous whistle you hear, is coming for you and you are only reassured when once the explosion has passed. That is real torture, for our 110 H.P. machines were not very easy to start. In the course of one of our flights to drive away these raiders, Prince and I were brought down one day, both of us having had our tank pierced with bullets. Luckily they were not incendiary.

In the first fortnight of September Hall, Prince and Rockwell each brought down an enemy plane. By this time the enemy was much less numerous and above all showed much less dash. The main body of his air forces had moved over to the Somme, where the Allied offensive was in full swing.

So ended for us the Battle of Verdun, which went down in the Escadrille's record, as the hardest struggle we had to face. The weather was constantly fine and the flying material but sparingly distributed, so that we had to use every machine until it was quite worn out. Every one had to fight with all his soul to hold his own against a tenacious foe.

In this task the Americans proved themselves the equals of the French soldiers of Caures Wood, of Pepper Hill, of Douaumont, of Dead Man's Hill, and of Hill 304. One can say no more.

Our Escadrille had become known throughout the world, but no one ever knew all that it did, for many of the planes we brought down we could not add to our record owing to lack of the necessary confirmation.   We had had 146 combats, 13 enemy planes, confirmed as having been brought down, one pilot killed and three wounded.   It was a fine record.

The authorities never spared the American Escadrille more than one of its own units, indeed the idea of such a thing would have humiliated us.   The Escadrille's baptism of fire at Verdun was an undying memory for all the pilots who took part in it, and later the survivors were wont to recall this terrible period when they had hardly time to sleep or eat, when they used to sleep fully dressed in their flying suits beneath their planes so as to be ready to start at the first glimpse of dawn.

Those were the heroic days of the Escadrille, its glorious prime.   Prince, Lufbery, Rockwell and Chapman, were you not worthy rivals of the greatest Heroes of any age or country?

CHAPTER IV

PARIS

Life on Leave—Return to Luxeuil—Kiffin Rockwell—
Norman Prince

On the 12th of September, 1916, the American Escadrille, which expected to use for winter quarters the comfortable Fougerolle Villa at Bar-le-Duc (Fougerolle was the owner's name), suddenly received orders to return to Luxeuil without machines. What did that mean? Everything was calm down there—it must be that Captain Happe had some plan in store and required our protection for his bombers. My pilots and I didn't worry much about the object of our future activity. We knew that there were no machines yet at Luxeuil, so the pilots asked me to pass by Paris on our way back there.

Lufbery was on leave when I received from him the following telegram: "Am held in prison at Chartres." I telephoned to the Officer in com-

mand at Chartres and learned that Lufbery had
broken six teeth of a railroad employee who had
been rude to him and knocked him out with the
same blow.   Lufbery was a pretty sudden propo-
sition when he was roused and moreover, in this
case, there was every excuse for him, for the
employee had been the first to lay hands on him,
which Lufbery regarded as an insult to his Military Medal.   I insisted on the importance of our
mission to the Commanding Officer and managed
to get my bird out of his cage.   You can imagine
how the others kidded him when he got back,
greeting him as "the jail bird."

In France the quickest way from one point to
another always leads through Paris.   As there
wasn't the least objection, I was glad to give the
pilots and myself the pleasure of a visit to the
capital.   What an attraction Paris has exercised
over all the fighting men during this war!

Who hasn't been to Paris?   Who hasn't gone
through it during these days of stress?   All the
peoples of the world have trodden its asphalt,
and the mixture of uniforms that mingled on its
Boulevards were a sight that will be unique for
ever.   It is well known that veteran soldiers have

a curious fatalism of their own and once danger is over they think of it no longer.   Did we even think of it while we were in the midst of it? Yes.   Yes, when we saw a dear friend disappear or when the Wings of Death brushed nearer us than usual.   But not for long; Life is stronger than Death.   Man is the only being who knows how to laugh and his natural gaiety springs ever to the surface.   Is not the sun stronger than the clouds which sometimes hide his face?

There can be nothing more restful for men who have been living for months at the war, not even daring to think that each day may be their last, than to get back to contact with the civilization of a great city.

Think how different was Paris from the spectacle we were accustomed to see.   No more butchery, no horrors, but among the yellowing chestnut trees of the Tuileries, the Autumn sun guilding the marbles, while in the Avenue spanned by the Arc-de-Triomphe, carriage after carriage sped swiftly by.

So, to visit Paris was considered a great favour, as regular leave every four months or more

seemed very long in coming.   Moreover, men on
regular leave were alone.   Doubtless they had
friends and acquaintances ready to take them
about and help them, but they felt lost without
their regular comrades.   The most devoted of
these friends of ours were unquestionably Mr.
Slade and his wife, Thaw's charming sister.
Everybody had recourse to them when it was a
question of breaking the news to a family who
had lost someone, or to reassure anxious hearts
far away across the Atlantic.   For all that, and
especially for all the other things they did for
my Escadrille, which I can't repeat for fear of
hurting their modesty, I wish to thank them.

We thought it a piece of wonderful luck to be
all together in Paris.   Despite the social difference between many members of the Escadrille,
there was a perfect understanding amongst them
on all subjects. "Esprit-de-Corps" smoothed
over any former differences that might have existed before, and rich or poor, educated or igno-
rant, professional men or manual labourers, they
all got on splendidly together.

Were they not all animated by the same spirit?

There were practically never any disputes, and it was very rare that I had to interfere as arbitrator. My own task was easy: I had simply to treat everyone fairly without prejudice or favour.

This good fellowship was maintained in Paris as at the front. Just as the toils and hard work of the front had been endured together, so the joys of Paris were shared in the best spirit of comradeship.

Generally, after a lazy morning, we would go to the Club before lunch to hear the news and meet the other French pilots on leave. When I say "Club" I mean the Hotel Chatham, where we would taste at the same time excellent Martinis, prepared by the expert hand of Santo.

As a regular thing, the American newspaper correspondents, who had come to consider themselves more or less as special war correspondents of the American Escadrille, would ply our pilots with questions, but the latter, well as they did their work, didn't care very much about speaking of it.

Sometimes, however, one of them, whose gaiety

had been stimulated by a well mixed Manhattan, would unblinkingly set going the most appalling "canards," which duly winged their way across the Atlantic. Thus, thanks to one of his pals, Thaw one day saw himself hailed as a hero by the newspapers of his native Pittsburg, for having landed in the enemy's lines and waged single-handed combat with a battery of Boche artillery, which he had reduced to silence with his machine gun! ! That was going it a bit strong.

However, all their stories were not jokes like this, and the best pilots, in the judgment of their peers, were quickly marked out for their renown to travel across the Atlantic.

Interesting fights, the brave deeds of those who had disappeared, the work that had been done, all this was related. Public opinion on the other side of the ocean wanted its own communiqué every day, a national communiqué, and it was the American Escadrille which supplied it.

Even the pro-German newspapers took note of us, and this publicity we received throughout the press was perhaps the best propaganda, for it showed to which side was attracted an élite,

animated solely by a noble purpose and a glorious
ideal. There was never an American Escadrille
in Germany.

But to return to Paris, and a good place too,
as my Americans would say. . . .

The morning never ended without our good
friend Mr. W. Moore Robinson gathering everybody, reporters and pilots, around his table, the
famous round table—were we not its modern
Knights? He used to offer us a last drink and
would generally hand over to our mess secretary
a coupon for fifty pounds of coffee.

Never did Mr. Robinson allow the Escadrille
to want for coffee. We thank him for his kindness. Afterwards we'd go off to lunch in little
groups and if anyone found himself too short of
money, the millionaires of the crowd, as we jok-
ingly called them, would be delighted to take him
along and stand him a lunch at the Ritz. It was
real good fellowship.

In the afternoon, the pilots interested in mechanics would go to the factories to have a look
at their future machines, and would give their
opinion as real connoisseurs, which was always
welcomed, especially regarding the shortcomings

of aeroplanes already in use. The engineers used to ask us what were our requirements. Later this was forbidden by the authorities, but it was thanks to this incessant collaboration, much more than to that of the offices, that constructors were able to make great improvements in their aeroplanes during the first years of the war.

But the best of good times must come to an end, and when the hour came to leave Paris we were all just as glad to go as we had been to arrive. Naturally our purses, which for every good American seemed to be simply his right hand pocket, were quite empty. We had once more to go after the Boche, everyone was ready without the least regret, and there was no falling off in the general high spirits.

It was on this trip that one morning Thaw read in the "Herald" that a Brazilian dentist wanted to sell a lion cub, bought on a visit to Africa. A syndicate was immediately formed to buy it with a capital of 500 francs. Its members were Prince, Thaw, Rockwell and Hall. The animal was to be the Escadrille's mascot. He was baptized "Whiskey." When Thaw appeared at the Gare de l'Est, with his animal on a leash, he took a dog's ticket and got into a carriage without any difficulty at first, but a controller came along. "What is that animal?" "An African dog," replied Thaw. But at that moment young Whiskey gave a loud roar and showed his claws. Some women jumped out of the carriage in terror, and the employee, enlightened as to Whiskey's true race, summoned the station master who forbade our friend to take the train. Thaw had to let the train leave without him and go and have a strong cage made for his "dog" and put it in the luggage car the next day. A lion in a luggage car—what a terrible come down from the Virgin Forest and the wilds of the bush! Finally, Thaw got the creature safely to Luxeuil, where it was received with open arms.

At the Pomme d'Or Hotel, Whiskey won the hearts of the two charming daughters of the proprietor, who put a pink ribbon round his neck and took great pains to find out what he liked best to eat. After several experiments, it was discovered to be bread and milk mixed. At first he used to show his claws on every occasion, but, after having received several good hidings, he learned to keep them covered, and soon became the best behaved of lions. He used to follow us like a dog, and would even accompany us for miles across country.

My dog, the famous Fram, the Escadrille's pet, a splendid and well trained police dog, adopted Whiskey as a pal, and it was wonderful to see them play together. They were such good friends that fifteen months later, when the lion was full grown, and could have easily eaten the dog up, they still played just as nicely, the only condition being that Whiskey wasn't interrupted with his meals.

To pass the time, while waiting for our machines, we used to fish for trout in the neighbouring streams or have parties with our friends from the Royal Navy. I remember one Homeric football match between British and Americans, played about midnight, with all lights out, in a shed belonging to the Englishmen. The walls yielded to our shoulders, and the players went head over heels outside. The reader can guess for himself the state of the furniture in the shed, and personally I was just as glad that the game had not been played in our own.

There were other less noisy amusements. At Luxeuil we organized dances in a big hotel and often used to dance one-steps and bostons, or teach our inexperienced partners the complicated steps of the tango or fox-trot. Finally, on the 19th of September, after a week's waiting, six machines reached us from the Bar-le-Duc reserve supply.

We set to work getting them ready, and the job was accomplished all the more quickly because they were Nieuport fifteen square meters, 110 H. P., fitted with Vickers Machine Guns, firing athwart the propellor with synchronization, and by this time our mechanics had more experience. Captain Happe didn't want to see us fly before the great mission for which we had come and whose date and object were still a mystery.

But think of restraining fanatics like Lufbery or Rockwell, when they had at their disposal superb new machines, fitted with the latest devices. On the 22nd, their machines were the first to be ready, and they were already flying over Mulhouse. On the 23d Lufbery and Rockwell were flying over Hartmannsweilerkopf just at the spot where the latter had won his first vic-

Presentation of flag to Lafayette Escadrille.

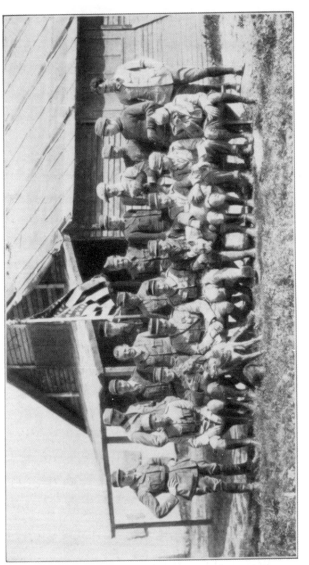

Presentation of Group (see Photo for names).

tory.   Up came a patrol of three Fokkers, who
manœuvred very skilfully.

I ought to say that on this Alsace front up to
1917, the Boche, rightly fearing bombardments
on factories, etc., behind their lines, had always
maintained a force of fighting planes superior to
our own, because for us it was a calm sector.
The enemy always had excellent pilots there with
the best and latest machines.   It was the easiest
place to attack them on their own ground, and
their population had a far greater fear of aerial
bombardments than our own.   Whereas in our
case our fighting planes were always sent to the
spot where an offensive was in progress.

Lufbery and Rockwell each attacked an adversary, but unfortunately Lufbery's machine-
gun jammed right at the beginning.   The first
trials of the Vickers machine-gun, as indeed of
all of them, were very unsatisfactory for us, constantly jamming, due especially to the drums and
the freezing of oil owing to the high altitude at
which we flew.   Only gradual improvements of
detail could set that right.

Lufbery had to beat a retreat and despite
clever manœuvres received three bullets in his

plane, one of which broke part of the framework of a wing.

He landed on the field of Fontaine, belonging to Escadrille 49. Rockwell followed him back to our lines, but didn't want to land and went back again to go on with his foray alone. It was dangerous, but that was Rockwell all over, and no one who knew his character could expect him to act otherwise. He was a born fighter and the blood of his soldier ancestors ran ever hot in his veins.

So he went back towards *"Old Armand,"* as our poilus call the Hartmannsweilerkopf, which they pronounced "Armand Fallières Kopf," and so "Old Armand."

About nine o'clock he perceived a solitary two-seater machine, a very swift little Albatross.

He dived headlong behind it without trying in his haste to place himself beneath it in the "dead" angle of its tail. Doubtless the enemy machine gunner had perceived him and, being well situated to fire, pulled trigger and hit him first in the head. Suddenly Rockwell's machine was seen falling out of control. The speed of his fall increased and as the motor was running full speed a wing broke off at about ten thousand feet. Rockwell fell about a mile from the lines, near the village of Rodern, where some artillerymen carried his body. Learning the news from the Rodern doctor, I immediately informed his brother Paul in Paris and sent a tractor to fetch the body.

From the ground, Lufbery was an impotent spectator of Rockwell's death, as well as that of the French Captain Munch, who had been brought down in flames at the same time almost over his own field.

Rockwell's brother arrived that night and the morrow we made a solemn pilgrimage to the spot where he had fallen. Cautiously, for the lines were close and the enemy could see us, the artillerymen led us to the exact spot where he had fallen in this plain of Alsace, where so many famous fights had been fought and where so many brave men had lost their lives. Greatly moved at the sight of the wrecked machine, we saluted and stood in silent prayer.

In the hope of taking our minds off this sad subject and especially for the sake of Paul Rockwell, who was utterly overcome at the thought of never seeing again his dearly loved brother, with whom he had shared the hardships of the Foreign Legion, I decided to drive home by Giromagny and the Ballon of Alsace. The wonderful grandeur of the scenery soothed our grief a little by giving us something else to think about.

With the same object I stopped at the crest of the Ballon for lunch. It was a warm day and we sat down at the foot of the monument of Jeanne d'Arc, Lorraine's greatest daughter, near a clear spring. Our hearts were very heavy, but nature all around us was full of life and sunshine and during so pitiless a war one had to force one's self to give way to sorrow.

The funeral took place on the 25th of September. All the civil and military inhabitants of Luxeuil were present. The townsfolk had stripped their gardens for flowers to deck our comrade's bier. In the cemetery, before the coffin, hidden beneath flags and flowers, it devolved on me to pay a last tribute to our dead friend. I could give no higher praise than to tell simply what he had done.

The following day Lufbery set out with redoubled ardour and as everything required had now arrived, the other pilots were also able to begin work.

Just at that time my turn for leave came round, so I went off to Biarritz, after having asked Captain Happe if he knew the date of our mission. As he replied that he didn't expect it would take place immediately, I felt free to go.

But on my way back, while passing through Paris on the 13th of October, I learned from the official communiqué that the expedition had taken place the preceding day against the Mauser factory at Oberndorf. What had happened? It appeared that orders to carry out the mission had come suddenly from headquarters on October 11th.

Sixty machines took part in it, slow Farmans, heavy Bréguets, with "pusher" propellors, old out-of-date planes flown by the French, accompanied by Sopwiths and still more Bréguets, flown by Canadian, Australian and South African pilots of the Royal Navy. Our four Nieuports flown by Lufbery, Prince, Masson and Lt. de Laage de Meux, who was in command of them, were to act as guards. The start couldn't take place until very late in the evening, as the bombing machines couldn't be got ready before. The planes flew off in sections, owing to the difference of speed. The Sopwiths, the best bombing planes in those days, carried out their mission without difficulty, but the Farmans, which were the first to start, were unable to make much height owing to their heavy load. The lines were crossed towards St. Dié to mislead the Germans. Unfortunately they were forced to pass no higher than 1200 feet from the ground as the hills in that neighbourhood were already three thousand feet above sea level. Adjutant Baron one of the most splendid pilots who ever flew, received a shell fair and square in his machine, which was blown to atoms.

"If I die," ran his last instructions, "do not grieve for me, but grieve for those who are left behind. It is more glorious to be dead than living in a war like this."

It took the bombing planes five hours to carry out their missions, and our Nieuports, who had only enough gas for two hours were instructed to escort them up to the Rhine in the region of Ettenheim, then go back and fill their tanks and return to meet them at the same spot on their way home.

The journey out went off all right, but as soon as our bomb planes were deprived of their protection, the Boches took advantage of this. However, losses were not too heavy, and the factories were set on fire by the famous Gros Bombs whose destructive power was terrible. They were composed of a mixture of two liquids (hydro-carbure and peroxide of azote). Our Americans went back to fill their tanks at Corcieux, according to plan, and then flew up again to seek their convoy; the latter, however, had scattered and the whole valley of the Rhine was a medley of aeroplanes, trying to reform and get back to our lines, pursued by Boche fighting planes. Unfortunately six French machines failed to return. Our pilots had little time that day to admire the beautiful scenery of the Rhine valley. Directly they reached it there was work for them to do. The bomb planes gathered round each of them for protection just as sheep huddle behind their faithful dogs when the wolf draws near.

Whenever an Albatros appeared a Nieuport

dashed upon him and put him to flight. So well did they work that several convoys were thus protected, each one by a single fighting plane.

The Boches finally gave up the struggle altogether after having lost some of their number from the machine gun fire of our pilots.

Prince was protecting the last of these convoys and refused to abandon it on any pretext whatever, for it had been entrusted to his care. The result was that by the time he got back to our lines it was already dark. The nearest aerodrome was Corcieux, a tiny field, situated in a hollow between lofty mountains. By day landing there was by no means easy, and in the darkness, when Prince made for it, there was no other illumination save a few cans of essence, whose contents had been spilt and set on fire.

Prince failed to see an electric power line bordering the field and capsized against the wires. He was picked up with both legs badly broken and behaved like a true hero, asking for news of his comrades and trying to sing so as to allay the anxiety of his rescuers. They bore him to the hospital of the Lake Hotel at Gerardmer, where the surgeons reported that there were good

Verdun in flames

The Fort of Thiaumont which changed hands ten times.
What is left of it after French and German bombardments.

grounds for hope.   On the morning of the 14th, I went to see him.   He had grown suddenly worse during the night.   I was deputed to confer on him the Cross of Chevalier of the Legion of Honour in the name of General Joffre, who had just granted it to him in recognition of the work he had done.

I gave it to him in his hospital cot, in the presence of Red Cross nurses, who were crying. His condition was desperate, as a result of a clot of blood on the brain.   He was dying of an embolism just when they were beginning to hope he was out of danger.

We were all terribly distressed at the thought of losing a friend so gentle and lovable and withal so brave, who had been the originator of the American Escadrille.   His two uncles arrived and could judge how hopeless was his case.

He passed away on Sunday morning, October 15.

The military funeral was held on the Luxeuil aviation field where the body rested on a caisson, draped with the American and French flags. The services were attended by a large representation of the Allied military divisions, including

French and English officers of high rank and a full representation of the American Escadrille and pilots from other aviation camps. The body was borne to a neighbouring chapel, there to rest until the end of the war, in accordance with military regulations.

A memorial service, held on the following Sunday in the American Church in Paris, was one of the most impressive ever held in that sanctuary.

It was the testimony of all Prince's comrades that they did not think he minded going. He wanted to do his part before he fell—and he had more than accomplished that purpose. He had engaged in 122 aerial engagements with enemy planes and he had been credited with five Boches, brought down in battle, not including others not officially recorded. He had successively achieved the ranks of sergeant, adjutant and lieutenant, and he had won all the emblems of distinguished service that France had to bestow— the Croix de Guerre, the Médaille Militaire and the Cross of Chevalier of the Légion d'Honneur.

The nobility of his character had endeared him to all who knew him. He was yet another American who had given his life for France. They were faithful unto death, these sons of the Land Across the Seas, just for the love they bore our country. How high his reputation stood in the army—even among the enemy—was illustrated by the chaplain at the funeral who was told by the commanding officer that he was anxious that Prince's death should not be known to the enemy —he was so valuable a flyer.

One of Prince's uncles said to me after the death of his brave nephew: "No, his death will not be in vain for hundreds of others in America will come to take his place. Even after his death he will be serving France." And it was true.

His brother, Frederick H. Prince, Jr., arrived too late to see Norman alive. At his request he was promptly transferred to his late brother's Escadrille, that he might take his place.

CHAPTER V

The Somme—Cachy Wood—Amiens—Winter

The losses, one after the other, had saddened our stay in Luxeuil. Now that our mission had been accomplished we were eager for a change, so Headquarters delighted us by giving orders that we should move to Cachy in the Department of the Somme, where almost all our fighting planes were concentrated. Masson, Lufbery and I flew over there, while our lorries accomplished the journey by easy stages.

The other pilots, who had no machines, took the train for Paris and on the 23rd of October we were all at Cachy. . . .

Cachy and its wood, how those words stand out in the story of French aviation. Never did our fighting planes do more glorious work than during that summer of 1916, both by the victories it won and by the fruits those victories bore.

Cachy evokes the names of Guynemer, Heurteaux, Dorme, Deullin, de la Tour, Vialet, Flachaire, Nungesser, Pinsard and a host of others, who there won undying fame.

The battle had begun on the 1st of July, although the struggle at Verdun was still in progress. Just as the Germans had made a great concentration of air forces for the latter operation, so Colonel Barès assembled yet larger and stronger forces for the Somme.

At Verdun the Germans had been unable to prevent us from recovering the upper hand in the air, with difficulty and at heavy cost it is true, but we had done it nevertheless during the month of March, thanks to our pilots who followed the example of Navarre and Boillot and were stimulated by the gallant Chaput, who once, when his machine-gun jammed, showed how to bring down a Boche without firing a shot. He had actually cut in half the body of his opponent's plane with his own propellor, a terrible risk to take. The American Escadrille had reached Verdun in May and our subsequent superiority was beyond question.

On the Somme, thanks to our "Aces" and our methods of fighting, the German aviation was distinctly outclassed from the beginning and lost more ground each day that passed. All the reports at that period go to prove that the German aviation was never able to pull itself together during the whole of this six months' battle. It was only when the bad weather of the Winter season gave them a breathing space that they were able to recover.

Those were fine times in the fighting service! Every day dozens of machines were brought down by our pilots. The English on their side were putting up a splendid performance. And our losses were light. Deullin had formulated a code of fighting tactics, which was exceedingly clear and simple. It gave magnificent results and may be summed up pretty much as follows:

1. Never attack without looking behind you.

2. Attack a single-seater from behind and above, then break the combat by a "chandelle," and *always maintain a superiority of altitude.*

3. Attack a two-seater by getting under its tail in the "dead" angle formed by the stabilizator, and stay there to prevent him taking you unawares.

4. Fly always waving around and break com-

bat when expedient by a clever "renversement."

Tireless, Guynemer and the rest flew as much as nine hours a day. They were bringing down Boches and one single Nieuport cleared the air around him. It was still the fine period of fighting for a lone pilot, who, moreover, was less likely than a patrol to alarm a foe who had been rendered cautious by many defeats.

A new machine of meteoric speed, 125 miles an hour, terror of novices, who spoke of it with bated breath, had just made its appearance. It was the Spad, which from the outset, handled by Guynemer and his comrades, literally pulverized the enemy.

So at Cachy we were going to keep high company and would have to put our best foot foremost if we wished to make a good showing against them. We were assigned to the group of Escadrille n° 13, commanded by Major Féquant, a leader who gave the example by never sparing himself in the least. We were destined to stay with him until the end.

We lost several days in going to fetch our machines, but at the end of the month we were able to begin our patrols.

An old fortune teller had foretold to Thaw that he would be brought down in October. This however didn't prevent him from accompanying me on a patrol on October 31st, when I was fortunate enough to hit a Boche plane which fell out of control in the enemy's lines south of Péronne.

All the same Thaw was pretty glad when he had landed. The month of October was passed and he was due to go on leave to the United States. The attraction of spending a fortnight in New York far outweighed the danger of all the Boche submarines.

Just at that time I received my first Spad with a 140 H. P. Hispano-Suiza engine. I was not a little proud of it; it worked magnificently and the engine was wonderful, easy to handle and developed speed unheard of at that epoch.

Unfortunately, fine days were growing few and far between and we were only able to fly occasionally.

The Somme is a foggy neighbourhood, and that particular winter from the 15th of November up to the 15th of January there weren't at the outside more than a dozen days suitable for

flying. Low fog and rain kept us continually
shut up in our wretched shed, hidden in Cachy
wood. What mud! What mud! 'twas enough
to make you think that all the quagmires of Po-
land, so dreaded once by Napoleon the First,
had made their rendezvous on the banks of the
Somme. To visit a neighbouring Escadrille, if
you left the duckboard you ran the risk of being
bogged or at least of leaving your boots in a
mud hole.

This time we had to see about our own quarters as well as continue our flying work. Pre-
viously the Escadrille had always been settled
very comfortably. Both at the Pomme d'Or Hotel and at the Bar-le-Due villa we had found
spacious kitchens and all the paraphernalia
needed. In Cachy Wood there was none of all
that, and without the kindness of neighbouring
Escadrilles we would have died of hunger. But
one never dies of hunger in France. The Stork
Escadrille n° 3, commanded by Major Brocard,
and Escadrille n° 67, commanded by Captain de
Saint-Sauveur, who had been on the spot for several months, were really exceedingly good to us.
Nevertheless, we had to get out and hustle our-

selves, and shortly after our arrival, Thaw asked me to let him go to Paris and make the necessary arrangements; I sent him with Masson. Thaw immediately went to Dr. Gros and with the help of the Escadrille's usual benefactors all the stuff, stoves, cooking utensils, etc., was quickly bought. There was no question of transporting all these goods by train, so a swift Ford, piloted by our good friend Allan Muhr, brought it all to Cachy.

Everything was now all right and our Escadrille's table at once acquired a well deserved reputation. A remarkable chef, who had been employed in embassies, if you please, was found in a neighbouring regiment. Our creature comforts were thus assured and not badly at that.

Then we all busied ourselves with the improvements of our quarters. As they stood they were really cheerless and penetrated by all the winds that blew. So the American shed soon re-echoed to the hammering of nails, as everybody set up barriers of matchboarding and woodwork against the cold and damp or made tables, washing-stands, etc. At this job the Americans were always the quickest to be thoroughly settled. Other Escadrilles managed perhaps to provide

more elaborate quarters, but they spent a great
deal more time over it.   However, there was one
thing here I would like to mention that surprised
me not a little:

One always hears people talk of the love of
comfort of the English and the Americans as
being greater than that of the French.   It is
false, absolutely false.   During this war I have
often seen the English and Americans put up
with the most primitive quarters without the least
attempt to improve them, whereas the French always tried to better their "wigwam."   Doubtless
because our people were more afraid of the cold,
but just the same they were thus better protected
against illness brought on by the winter.   In the
French climate the Anglo-Saxon races are much
more liable than we are to bronchitis and pneu-
monia.   An American who had lived in the
North of France for several years once said to
me: "I used to laugh heartily at the French
dread of draughts, but now I believe you are
right.   The customs of a country should always
be respected."

As regards food it was much the same as for
quarters.   Taking it by and large it is my opin-

ion that the French soldier was the best fed and for this reason he had the best cooks. Take any Frenchman and make him a cook and he'll turn you out something eatable. It isn't the same with the English and the Americans. However, they can appreciate good food just as much as we can, but in default of it they seem to get along quite happily.

The question was what to do in the long winter evenings. We used to sit and warm ourselves around the stove. It was a great joy when the American mail came in, sacks full at a time. The whole big table was hidden under the pile of American newspapers and their ever-interesting supplements.

One of our favourite pastimes was to hunt in these newspapers for anything about the Escadrille. The papers of New York, Chicago and Pittsburg used all of them to "play up" those pilots who were their fellow-townsmen. We were also not a little interested in reading about the great doings of fake American aviators! Their "gallant deeds" were told at great length and there were full details of receptions given in their honour. Generally they had never even crossed the Atlantic! ! !   This used to make my pilots absolutely furious and if they could have laid their hands on one of these imposters he would have fared pretty badly.

Some of our fellows used to write their memoirs, others would start a mild game of poker, or begin throwing dice upon the table, accompanying their game with ferocious cries. Artists would decorate the walls of the room with original drawings, representing air battles. Genet was the best at this kind of work.

But I don't know what would have become of us without the gramophone. We had two very good ones and Hill had brought back from America a whole series of excellent records, so that the strains of fox-trot or rag-time alternated with airs from French or Italian operas according to the taste of the individual.

Lufbery preferred strange melodies, often melancholy in character, which are, it appears, very popular in America. It was Hawaiian music, tunes played by a sort of banjo called Ukelele.

These tunes were generally very beautiful and

in listening to them Lufbery used to dream of the distant strands where he had lived and their spreading palm trees. But the note of melancholy was quickly forgotten and Lufbery himself was the first to shake it off in telling some of his innumerable experiences of travels far and wide.

Lufbery used to tell us of his life of adventure, his wanderings across the world. A mere boy, he had left France, where he had been brought up, and travelled over Europe, Turkey and India. For a living he did what came to hand, often changing his occupation. Hoping to travel more he enlisted for three years in the American army, and visited Hawaii and the Philippines. After its discharge he wandered to Calcutta at a time when Marc Pourpe came there to give aeroplane exhibitions. The latter one day advertised in a local newspaper for a mechanic. Lufbery, who had never seen an aeroplane motor in his life, volunteered for the job. "I know nothing about it," he said, "but I'll learn quick." He became the faithful comrade and friend of Pourpe, whom he accompanied on a flying trip through the Sudan to Khartoum.

On the outbreak of war Pourpe having been mo-
bilized as a pilot, Lufbery stayed with him as
mechanic.   Pourpe was killed and Lufbery became a pilot to avenge him.

We were delighted with his stories, and then
when he stopped the phonograph would begin
again its twangy song, and the ardent dancers
among us would give vent to the restlessness of
their feet by performing a clog dance with their
heels rapping a saraband on the floor.

One day we made a trip to the trenches and
when we got home, after comparing their life
with that of the infantry, all the pilots decided
that they were relatively fortunate and expressed
their loud admiration for the humble toil of the
men who ever mounted guard before No Man's
Land.   They had seen too the ruin that had been
spread over our country, the wounded earth rendered barren for many years to come.   One of
the things that struck them the most was to have
seen in the cemetery of Dampierre all the tombs
torn open, profaned, violated and transformed
into "abris."   The dead were dead indeed, why
could not the Germans let them sleep in peace?

Sometimes—and this was a very different

story—we took at nightfall, which came early in December, the road for Amiens, which was only about six miles away. Amiens was the rendezvous for the French and British Armies. Crowds of soldiers in every variety of uniform thronged its streets and shops, to say nothing of the cafés, bars, and tea-shops.

The English element was in majority at the Savoy Bar or at Charley's, but there was the best of good fellowship between them and the French, to which our Americans were immediately admitted. In this connection I remember that one very dark night in a street that was darker still there appeared before us on our way out of Amiens a soul in pain. He was lying right beneath our feet at the foot of an extinguished lamp. Investigation revealed that he was a Scotchman, for he was wearing the famous tartan breeches.

It was cold and raining heavily. We couldn't leave him there, for certainly an M. P. would have roped him in and he'd have got into trouble.

It was quite out of the question to ask him what unit he belonged to, for he was far past

Campbell's Nieuport after landing with a wing missing,

Lt. Verdier.

Funeral of Hoskier.   His Mother, Father, the Minister.

speech. It took but a moment to install him in the bottom of our car and so we took him off to Cachy Wood.

There I fixed him up comfortably on a camp bed, where he slept until noon the following day. One cannot imagine the utter stupefaction of the Scot when he awoke to find himself surrounded by men wearing French uniforms but speaking English!!!

His first words were: "What, I've been taken prisoner?"

It was then our turn to be surprised. For the moment nothing we could say would alter his opinion. He thought he was in German territory as a result of some mysterious mishap, all memory of which had passed from his mind. He was convinced that we were spies instructed to make him talk, and accordingly refused to tell either his regiment or the spot where it was located. The situation was really too ridiculous.

At last I said to him in desperation: "You're free, don't you understand, free; you're with the American Escadrille, which is fighting in the French army. It was rather a shock to our self-esteem to learn that he had never even heard of us. But in the end we persuaded him to listen to reason.

After having visited our hangars and taken lunch with us—his appetite was conspicuously poor—I lent him a car to take him back to his camp. He was a nice fellow, I believe a well-known golfer, but I hope he will forgive me for having forgotten his name.

Soubiran, Haviland and Frederick Prince joined the Escadrille at this time. The latter, who had come to take his brother's place, was transferred to Pau as an instructor in the aviation school.

We used to profit by the few glimpses of fine weather, but the Boche was very scarce; he was quietly reorganizing for the Spring and paid no attention to our efforts to draw him out.

However, he did make up his mind to carry out some bombing raids on occasional fine nights, for often after sunset the sky would grow clear.

We had long set the enemy an example and finally he resolved to imitate us, and I must admit that two of his first efforts met with pretty fair success.

Once he burnt a hangar fifty yards from our shed and its contents, a dozen Spads, went up in flames.   It was a hangar of the Stork Escadrille and Guynemer's machine was amongst those destroyed.   However a new one was ready for him the following day.

Another enemy plane set fire to a huge munition dump at Cerisy-Gailly.   Every one who fought on the Somme will remember this extraordinary "firework" display; a million shells exploded.   It was a pretty good reply to the blow we had given the Germans some weeks before in the neighbourhood of St. Quentin, when one of their dumps was bombed and its explosions were heard to continue for three days.

We tried to attack enemy raiders by night, very dangerous work for such swift planes as ours.   De Laage and Pavelka were especially ardent on these occasions.

It was at this moment that I chose the Indian's Head as insignia for our machines and soon there was no more popular emblem in all the flying world.   The savage Sioux with his threatening expression, drew all eyes to the body of the plane on which it was painted.   It was

moreover a real work of art. Willis perfected
and gave its final form to the sketch that had
been first drawn by the mechanic Suchet.

Towards the beginning of November we received the following curious message from the
Minister of War: "For diplomatic reasons Escadrille 124 will henceforth be called the Volunteer Escadrille. It is expedient to abandon the
title 'American Escadrille.'"

The reason for this was as follows: so-called
Americans resident in Germany had complained
that we had bombed them in the towns where
they were staying. Bernstorff had made a protest to Washington. The charge was false. To
begin with no American had made a complaint
and secondly we had never done any bombing
but had always worked as fighting planes. But
France, being anxious to avoid diplomatic inci-
dents on her account between the United States
and Germany, was particularly careful to maintain a line of conduct that was perfectly correct.
We were furious, but happily we were to have
our revenge. Thanks to Dr. Gros and Captain
Berthaud, attached to the Ministry of War, we

Fire caused by Boches on our Senart field.

Fire caused by Boches on our Senart field.

The Kaiser holds a council of war after the battle of Malmaison. Note his withered arm. Behind him the. Crown Prince.—Hindenburg in the middle.

All look anxious. (Photograph found on the body of a German officer).

received a new message as follows: "6th December, 1916. The Minister of War announces that the Volunteer Escadrille will henceforth be called the 'Lafayette Escadrille.'"

This announcement was communicated to every Escadrille in France and henceforth we were never known by any other name. Our insignia, as well as the name of the Escadrille, indicated frankly and boldly the origin of our pilots. The Germans could never have had the least doubt on the subject.

The gloomy Winter dragged on. . . . Ah, Péronne, Sailly-Saillisel, Bouchavesnes, Chaulnes, how dreary it was to fly above your ruins, the sun ever hidden and your sites so pockmarked with water-filled shell craters as to give appearance of a country in the moon.

Imagine our joy when we got a really fine day on December 27th. Every one was out fighting from the earliest hours, and Lufbery profited by the occasion to bring down an enemy plane south of Chaulnes. In the morning he had missed another through his machine gun jamming, and had received no less than seven bullets in his own plane during the battle. Just at that moment Guynemer brought down a Boche quite close to Lufbery.

Then came the frost, very severe frost. There was no more mud but we had enough to worry about with the motors of our Spads. To begin, there were no protective shutters for the radiators. We had to find some means of supplying the deficiency ourselves, and put it into practice, which took a lot of time. The ground was so hard as a result of the frost that the tires of our wheels burst at every landing. Luckily the Boche was still very inactive.

On the 24th of January, Lufbery brought down yet another enemy and our junior pilots learned skill from his example. Thaw too had returned from America and was getting busy. Hoskier joined us at the beginning of December and Genet and Parsons towards the end of January. On January 26th we moved over to Ravenel near St. Just-en-Chaussée. It was to begin the preparation of a new offensive which was to take place in the Spring. We had instructions to show ourselves as little as possible in this sector so as not to attract the attention of the enemy, and, as the Boches were as much hampered by the cold as we were, the month of February was exceedingly quiet.

The rupture of diplomatic relations between the United States and Germany gave us food for conversation, although great differences of opinion existed amongst my pilots as to what was likely to follow. President Wilson was sending his Notes to the Germans. Although we did not see clearly his motives, the President knew what he was about. He was determined to neglect no chance of conciliation, however small it might be, instead of throwing his people headlong into the vortex. My pilots were too impatient to understand fully the prudence that must accompany great responsibilities.

We were much more disturbed over the cold. Everything that would burn went into the stove and once we had read the bulky Sunday editions there was no question what to do with them. Thaw's young brother Blair, who two years later was to give his life for his country had chosen this moment to pay a visit to his brother at the Escadrille. He couldn't stand the terrible cold in our matchboard sheds and we had to send him back to Paris suffering from high fever.

To warm himself Soubiran used to go hunting the numerous partridges and hares of the neighbourhood and it was not uncommon to see him suddenly dash breathless into the shed, hastily hide his gun, plunge under the bed clothes and appear to be sound asleep. That meant that the forest rangers were after him hot and heavy, for hunting was forbidden. But our Chef did make such delicious jugged hare!

We had managed to get a piano at the town of Clermont, and Bigelow, playing with all his might, with the same idea of keeping warm, used to give us his whole répertoire with inimitable talent. On the 23rd of February Lufbery received the Cross of the Legion of Honour and we made a great celebration. A banquet was given to the Lafayette Escadrille over which Major Féquant presided. At the end of the month Willis, Lovel and Hinkle joined the Escadrille; the latter fell sick and only remained with us a short time. The other two subsequently became excellent pilots.

Training.

Training.

The last patrol of Mac Connell.

Lowell.   Genet.   Lufbery.   Mac Connell.

Ham Aerodrome.

CHAPTER VI

Spring and renewed activity—General advance—Losses—
Ham—Chaudun—Battle of the Aisne

Our rest was drawing to an end and a period
of very hard work about to begin. The Boches,
who had been badly hammered by the soldiers
of Joffre during the Battle of the Somme, were
beginning their preparations for retreat towards
St. Quentin and the famous Hindenburg line,
and we were the first to perceive it. Villages
and depôts were being burned and it was sad to
see the houses of my fair France thus destroyed.
Another indication,—rails were being taken up
and the artillery fire was diminishing. Our
work grew to be uninterrupted for we had to obtain exact information as to the enemy's inten-
tions.

The Boche thought to interfere with our offensive that was being prepared on the Mont-
didier front by an "elastic retreat" upon very

strong positions that had been carefully prepared and against which they hoped our strength would be shattered.   It was not such a bad idea.   But we did not fall into the trap and immediately began to dig new trenches when we reached the outskirts of their fortified lines.

On the 15th of March our artillery bombarded the Boches who were left in their first lines with the object of starting our advance.   Our troops went forward under the command of General Nivelle, who had succeeded General Joffre.

For some days the whole army thrilled with new enthusiasm.   To go forward after months of stagnation, what joy for all the soldiers and for all France.   It seemed to every one that we would never stop before the Rhine, or at least on the Meuse.   Our chiefs, however, and especially the aviators, knew that the Hindenburg line was very formidable with its stretches of barbed wire in some places literally miles deep. The German retreat took place during the night, by day the roads were deserted and it was in vain we looked for convoys that we might scatter them with our machine guns.   We never saw any.

On the 17th of March in the small hours of the morning, while it was still dark, I was awakened by the telephone. Zeppelins were making for Paris, passing by Compiègne. Without losing an instant we set off in pursuit and reached Compiègne just in time to see one brought down in flames by artillery fire. What a glorious torch it made as it fell, and what a thrilling sight was this long reptile, twisted and burnt, as it lay smashed upon the ground.

That day too the French made a big jump forward in their pursuit of the enemy.

At this time the Tsar abdicated in Russia, but already we had begun to feel that the entry of America into the war was at hand. Not only had diplomatic relations been broken but the current of bold and generous ideals was flowing strong. As my pilots said to me joking: "Captain, you're going to be replaced, you will soon be no longer the Commander-in-Chief of the Americans—General Pershing is coming soon to succeed you in your high office." How I rejoiced for my country's sake that the Americans were coming in.

On the 16th of March Thaw went to Paris

to get a Spad. He took with him Whiskey, now grown big, to consult an oculist, for our poor lion had had an eye knocked out by a blow of a stick by Rumsey.

Our idea was to have them give him a glass eye, but Thaw had no luck. All the doctors to whom he applied—were far too frightened to hear of it. And yet we were prepared to pay heavily to restore to our lion his former æsthetic appearance.

With the veterinaries Billy had no better success. He then went to the Zoological Gardens, where the keepers were all frightend and couldn't believe their eyes at seeing a lion cub permit himself to be handled like that and playing with the dog Fram which Thaw had taken along. With animals much smaller than Whiskey they took many precautions. "You are a wonderful lion tamer," they said to Thaw, but they too declined to have anything to do with the operation.

As it happened a lioness had lately had cubs and Thaw took advantage of this to buy a companion for our mascot. Could we give our new acquisition any other name but "Soda"?

On the 18th Thaw flew back on his Spad and had his menagerie transported to the Escadrille in cages.

The 19th of March was a stirring day for us, De Laage and Thaw made a magnificent scouting trip over St. Quentin, diving down at each doubtful spot, at each clump of trees, at each village to be met by bullets betraying when they were occupied. They were warmly congratulated by Commander Féquant. Then Genet and MacConnell went out in turn. Between Ham and St. Quentin they were attacked by several enemy planes. MacConnell didn't come back and was reported "missing." Genet's account ran as follows: "With Sergeant MacConnell, entered enemy's lines north-east of Ham, and made towards St. Quentin. At Douchy three enemy planes flying above us attacked. While fighting with one of them who fired incendiary bullets at me I lost sight of MacConnell. I hit my enemy, but during this time the third Boche opened heavy fire upon me from a distance of 25 yards and cut a strut, one of my wingtip controls and wounded me in the left cheek. No longer seeing MacConnell, I made back to our lines, where

I awaited him fifteen minutes above Ham.
North of Ham villages were burning and from
the same region too a battery opened fire upon
me."

Poor Jimmy! We were all so fond of him.
Looking at the first photograph taken at Luxeuil
of the first five members of the Escadrille, three
of whom, Chapman, Rockwell and Prince, had
already disappeared, MacConnell, who with me
was the only survivor, once said to me: "It is
my turn next, and it would have been better that
I had been killed rather than Chapman. He
would have done better work than I for he was a
cleverer pilot."

What a modest fellow he was, and what a
noble spirit of calm philosophy was taken from
us at his death. And when I look at the tragic
photograph, as we used to call it, in which I
alone am left alive, my heart is very heavy at
the thought of my brave comrades.

MacConnell's exact fate only became known
to us a few days later.

This same day of the 19th. Thaw, who had
landed at Nesles in front of our vanguard, had
trouble with his motor and couldn't start off

again. Luckily the Boches had no thought of offensive action and were filled with the idea of running to earth in the Hindenburg line.

To repair Thaw's motor we had to pass through an army on the move, which was not easy, owing to the choked condition of the roads, many of which had been rendered useless by the enemy. The job was done by the help of Soubiran, who had once been mechanic in the celebrated Indianapolis races. At Roye the road had been destroyed by vast mine craters and all the trees bordering it were cut, sawn almost wholly through so that they stood upright only by force of habit, as it were, and were brought down on the road by the slightest breeze.

Words cannot describe the joy of the inhabitants who embraced us now that an end had been put to their sufferings, their long martyrdom with its fines, prison, deportations and thousand and one other vexations, which they had to relate. In later days such a sight was to be all too familiar to American fighters also.

On March 24th I took my Spad and landed near Ham. There I asked for an automobile, and went from Division to Division, asking if any one had news of Jim MacConnell. Finally I learned that a machine had been reported in a field by the road from Bois L'Abbé to Petit Detroit about a mile and a half south of Jussy. I managed to get there not without difficulty, for the Germans were still just on the other side of the canal. It was indeed MacConnell's Nieuport with its emblem. Beside it lay his body, which had been taken out of the machine. All his papers had been removed and the Germans had even carried off his boots.

With the aid of Major Uffler of the 48th Battalion of Chasseurs à pied, I managed to get him a decent burial. Beside a little French by-way a simple cross invites the passer-by to stop and devote a thought, a memory, to the brave forerunner of America's armies, who lies buried there.

At Ravenel we were then too far away from the front, at least forty miles, so we established ourselves at Ham on a field formerly used by the enemy.

At this time Ham had not suffered very much, as unfortunately has been its case since. It was very different with the neighbouring villages, which had been completely and deliberately de-

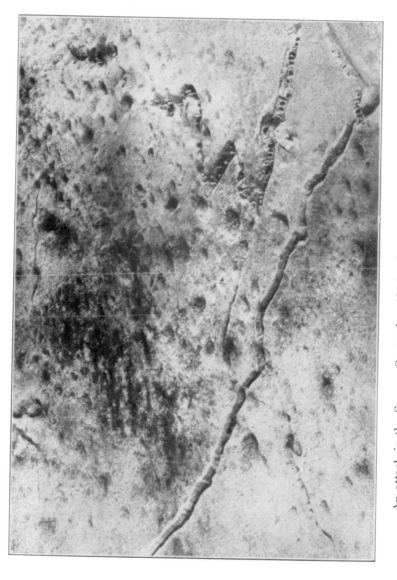

An attack in the Somme September 1916.　One sees the men in the trenches.

The Somme — the attack September 1916.

Chaulnes — oblique view.

stroyed by the Germans. In Ham about two-thirds of the houses were uninjured, but the bridges had been destroyed and the cross-roads and public squares were nothing but huge craters torn open by the explosion of mines.

The Germans had more or less spared these small towns because they assembled the population of each canton in its principal town. The rest of the villages were systematically destroyed, the walls overthrown by means of special battering rams, the fruit trees cut down and the wells poisoned by throwing manure into them.

The historic castle of Ham, where Louis Napoleon Bonaparte, afterwards Napoleon III, had been in prison during the reign of Louis-Philippe, was utterly razed to the ground by several mines. What a barbarous act to destroy these stones a thousand years old without any military reason. It was simply the fury of destruction which had animated these modern Huns. So too had been destroyed the celebrated Castle of Coucy.

At Ham William Dugan and Kenneth Marr, who subsequently did very good work, joined the Escadrille. Thomas Hewitt also joined us there.

On the 8th of April Lt. de Laage brought down two enemies one after the other north of St. Quentin, thus relieving the pressure on some English planes who were in a hot fight. This exploit, added to all that he had done before, won for him the Legion of Honour, granted on April 21st. It was well deserved by this true leader of men, whose courage and bearing always gave him a remarkable influence over all who came in contact with him. Unfortunately, a time of cruel losses was coming for the Escadrille. On April 16th young Genet was killed in full flight by a shell south of St. Quentin. He was one of our best pilots, the type of man who always had to be restrained rather than encouraged; always ready to sacrifice himself.

I see no harm in relating here that to be accepted in the Foreign Legion, in which he had first served France, Genet had told a pardonable falsehood. He hadn't reached the age required for all who wished to volunteer for the Legion, so he had deliberately added three years to his age to make it twenty-one. Brave Genet! Sleep in peace in the France you loved so well!

He was the first American to be killed since his country had declared war. The American Embassy in Paris was represented at his funeral by Mr. R. W. Bliss and Mr. Ben Thaw, our pilot's brother.

Beside Genet in the cemetery of Ham was all too soon to lie his comrade Hoskier, a splendid high-souled fellow, whose only thought was to fight for the cause that was sacred to him. He had the spirit of his father who was still fighting at Verdun. With Madame Hoskier the latter reached Ham just in time to take part in the last sad honours to their son.

I can give Hoskier no higher praise than to say he was a second Chapman. The same fire animated them both. General Franchet d'Esperey granted him the following citation: "Ronald Wood Hoskier, American citizen, volunteer in the service of France, the true soul of a hero both in bravery and spirit of sacrifice. Fell the 23rd of April after heroic defence in a fight against three enemy machines."

With Hoskier fell the Frenchman Dressy, the faithful orderly of Lt. de Laage. He had asked

as a favour to accompany Hoskier as machine-
gunner in a two-seater.   It was the only machine
of this kind we had in the Escadrille.

They were attacked by three enemy planes and
brought down south of St. Quentin near the first
line.   Dressy had begun the war with de Laage
in a regiment of Dragoons.   He had accompanied him as a matter of course on a dangerous
patrol, when the officer had his horse shot under
him and his leg pierced by a bullet.   Dressy dis-
mounted and under a hail of projectiles tenderly
placed de Laage on his own horse, jumped up
behind him and brought him back safe to our
lines.

De Laage was deeply grieved, as were we all,
at the loss of his good comrade in arms who had
saved his life.   Some one has said that those
who are true friends seem to follow each other
closely to the grave by a sort of mysterious bond.
On the 23rd of May, de Laage was trying a new
machine on the Ham field.   He had just left the
ground, when the motor suddenly stopped running at a height of 250 feet and the machine
crashed heavily to earth.   We hurried to the spot.
De Laage had ceased to live.   This accident oc-

The American Escadrille at Verdun.

After the bombardment.

Thaw, though wounded, comes back
to the Escadrille.

curred frequently because the high compression
motors we employed were not yet fitted with a
suitable carburetor, but it was our duty to fly
whether we were killed or not—it was war and
we could not forget it.

Our grief was very great: for me de Laage
was a true friend, and if one is saddened by the
death of a comrade, how bitter is the distress
when one loses a friend. For more than a year
we had shared troubles, toils and pleasures, and
suddenly he was gone, leaving a void that nothing could fill.

Ham gave him an imposing funeral and in
the cemetery above his grave I repeated his last
words, a splendid epitaph for a soldier: "Since
the formation of the American Escadrille, I have
tried to exalt the beauty of the ideal which
brought my American comrades to fight for
France. I thank them for the friendship and
confidence they always shown me. If I die do
not weep for me. It is not good that a soldier
should let himself give way to sorrow and now
'Vive la France!'"

Why was it that we had always thus to steel
our hearts against regrets and why, as MacCon-

nell said, "was it always the best who get killed?"
Truly this war was dreadful and pitiless.   One
could never stop to grieve.   In the mêlée men had
to throw themselves one after another like num-
bers without individuality and yet God knows
they did not lack character, these French and
American heroes.   It was necessary.   It is the
law of war that, no matter what kind hearts too
filled with sentimentality may write, only the
will of the leader, who sets aside pity that might
lead to weakness, can conquer.   "No, War is no
mere game"—for once Bernstorff had spoken the
truth.

"Do not lose time in lamenting me," de Laage
had said, and if the wound still bled at the bottom of our hearts we must hide our sorrow and
continue our work with unflagging spirit.

And there was work to do.   The Boche, who
in 1916 had been distinctly beaten as far as
aviation was concerned, had carried out during
the winter an enormous program of production under the direction of General Groener.   In
the Spring the enemy brought out a great number of Albatros D.3 and D.5 single-seater ma-

chines superior to anything he had had up till then. Luckily the Spad was inimitable.

The enemy had also instructed a great number of pilots and, reaping the fruits of all his preparations, he became singularly aggressive. His "flying circuses" appeared everywhere and attacked our artillery observation planes. We gave them this name on account of their habitual tactics. Seven or eight Albatros would fly in a circle of great circumference, round and round like horses in the ring at a fair. Woe to the rash pilot who attacked one of them. The German, who was thus attacked, dived towards the interior of the circle and broke the combat by a sudden manœuvre while his assailant was attacked in turn, in an unfavourable position, by another enemy, the next in order of the circle.

In attacking a circus one had to make a single dive at one's opponent without getting down below the level of the circle, then break away by a vigorous "chandelle" towards the exterior, giving full power to his engine. If the enemy was not brought down in the first attack the only thing to do was to get away quick, as I have said, without attempting to carry on the fight under penalty of being one's self brought down.

It was at this time too that the Boche commenced the tactics of coming to harass the infantry with their machine-guns before dawn. In the night beyond reach of attack they would worry our soldiers, who had given them the name "Fantomas." We tried to fight them, and it was a strange sight to see our Spads go off in the middle of the night. Owing to its speed and its complete lack of the "vol-plané," the Spad was far from being a perfect machine for night flying. If only no motor trouble came before daylight! That was always our fervent hope. On one of these flights a French comrade named Allez had his depth controls completely cut by a shell in full career. He managed to land without great harm by switching off and on his motor so that he descended in a series of falls. It was yet another case of a man coming back from the gates of death.

Doubtless night fighting gave no results, but the noise of our motors pleased the infantry and completely reassured them. We could see so little that one day, or rather one night, we made a

Senart aviation camp.

Lufbery's Spad struck by shell.

Lufbery and his lions Whiskey and Soda.

patrol flight with a machine which had joined us and it was only at the first streaks of dawn that I perceived it bore the hated black crosses instead of our friendly tricolor. We attacked him but he did not wait for battle and fled at full speed.

To clip the claws of our enterprising enemy Lufbery, Thaw, Haviland and Johnson successively brought down an aeroplane apiece in the same week.

On April 16th, the Allies began their great offensive on the Aisne and in Champagne. The first day we got very satisfactory results—33,000 prisoners. Unfortunately, the tanks, which we were using for the first time, and moreover in small number, were not yet in fighting trim and many burnt up with their gallant crews, their gasoline containers being insufficiently protected. The enemy was considerably reinforced by all the Divisions he had brought back from Russia, and so he reacted violently and set himself to retake from us piecemeal what we had captured en bloc. From the point of view of aviation it was in this latter fighting that the struggle was most severe, especially for us as we were not far distant from the scene of action and were constantly requested to patrol thereabouts.

During this fighting, Andrew Courtney Campbell joined the Escadrille and some time afterwards there befell him one of the most astounding adventures that ever happened to any pilot, an adventure which made a great stir throughout the French flying world. He used to be very fond of acrobatic "stunts" and perhaps had strained his machine somewhat. Anyway one day, flying a Nieuport at about 45,000 feet, his lower left wing broke right away, fluttered down and fell into the forest of Villers-Cotterets, where it never was found.

The wing was broken off clean, just level with the body and at the points of junction with the struts. Not a bit of it was left on the plane.

With this machine, biplane on the right and monoplane on the left, Campbell succeeded in coming down and landing intact near our aerodrome in a field of beetroots. How did he manage? It was a perfect miracle that the remaining wing did not yield in its turn, thus plunging Campbell to certain death.

After the accident all the learned experts of

the aviation came along to study such an incredible case and prove that it was possible to fly in these conditions.   None the less it took a man like Campbell with his iron nerve to carry out this exploit which remains unique in the annals of aviation.

On the 3rd of June, continuing our wanderings from sector to sector, we had gone to the aerodrome of Chaudun, half way between Villers-Cotterets and Soissons, right in the Chemin des Dames sector.   During our stay at Ham the record had been 66 pitched battles, 7 enemy planes brought down, three of our pilots killed and one wounded.   As usual directly that a sector began to get calm we left it.   Perhaps the reader is surprised by the comparatively small number of battles that ended in a plane being brought down.   Not only is not so easy to bring down an enemy plane—and one must always remember that the foe has a chance of victory just as you have—but the French have always been very strict as regards the confirmation of victories and have always required that an enemy's fall be recorded by land observation.   I am sure that the number of enemy planes brought down was in reality much greater than our records showed. To give a definite proof of his victories—in cases where the fight was too far behind the enemy lines to be recorded—Guynemer had ended by fixing on his Spad a photographic apparatus and in some cases had brought back photographs of his victims in pieces or in flames.

In this sector as in those before, Lufbery continued to distinguish himself. He had just been decorated with the English Military Medal by His Majesty King George V and in a formal session the Aero-Club of France had just granted him its grand gold Medal. On the 21st of June he was promoted officer, Second Lieutenant in the French army. For all his modesty the former globe-trotter was very proud of it.

We were then joined by Bridgman, Drexel, Dolan, Jones, Peterson, Mac-Monagle and James Hall, an excellent lot of pilots. They set themselves to follow in Lufbery's footsteps, and what with their own qualifications and an example like his they fully maintained our standard.

James Norman Hall who had volunteered as infantry machine-gunner in the English army had been wounded and invalided from the serv-

Faubourg-St. Leonard.—Nesles.

Note roofs damaged by explosion mine at cross roads.

Roye.—Nesles.—road cut by mines.

Funeral of Genet.—The Minister.

Funeral of Hoskier and Dressy.

ice. He then enlisted in the French army as pilot. He was brave to a degree that bordered on rashness. On the 26th of June, while attacking single-handed seven enemy planes over the Chemin des Dames during a violent German offensive, he was brought down in the French lines in the Ravine of Ostel with his breast pierced right through. The gallant fight he had made had won cheers of applause from the French troops, themselves engaged in a bitter struggle, and contributed not a little to that day's victorious resistance. The Crown Prince's troop had received orders to hurl the French at all costs back into the Aisne. I drove over to fetch Hall and it was no easy job on account of the very heavy bombardment. Naturally we ran with all lights out, the rows of camions followed one another and at places crossed each other, the teams of horses galloped in the most dangerous spots and to drive in the midst of it all in utter darkness took a good deal of nerve and plenty of confidence in one's luck. Our chauffeur was rather upset by the continual shell bursts, as the enemy fired systematically on all the routes of communication to interfere with the flow of supplies. This used to be called harassing fire. Doubtless our batteries were playing the same game with the enemy, but from our particular point of view that was no compensation. Soubiran once more came to our rescue by taking the driving wheel. Hall had already been picked up, and we found him at the hospital of Mont Notre Dame.

The tractor which I sent the following night to get the wreckage of Hall's machine, was set on fire by a shell, but nobody was wounded.

I proposed Hall for the Military Medal, which was immediately granted him.

Just as when Guynemer had been made Officer of the Legion of Honour, his citation had mentioned the enthusiasm that his dare-devil courage had aroused among the troops in the trenches. Less than five months afterwards Hall came back to take his place in the Escadrille. What a splendid soldier he was! After having distinguished himself in the British and French armies, he was to become once more conspicuous for gallantry in the American army. Few men have fought as real combatants in three armies and he must hold a unique record.

On the 4th of July there was once again a great celebration in Paris at the statues of Washington and Lafayette. A delegation was there to represent the Escadrille, and a big luncheon was given in our honour.

On the 7th of July right in the middle of the battle the Lafayette Escadrille received its flag, and the whole French Aviation was summoned to this ceremony on the field of Chaudun.

A Battalion of Chasseurs-à-pied—the Blue Devils—was also present and its band played during the march past, while from the hands of Commander Du Peuty, at that time the gallant chief of the French Aviation, killed a short while afterwards in a charge at the head of his infantry battalion, Thaw received the Star Spangled Banner, embroidered by the hands of Mrs. MacAdoo and the women employees in the Treasury Department at Washington. The Tricolor bowed before the starry flag, the bugles sounded "Au Drapeau," and every one felt that it was France saluting America.

There was as yet no more than a band of twenty-five pilots grouped in our humble shed, but the future was already big with the preparation of numberless air phalanxes which were training far over there. We had promised to carry this flag on high in all our battles. With pilots like mine I had no anxiety; the promise would be kept.

It was at this time that the Escadrille had its greatest number of pilots, but in view of their continuous arrival Headquarters decided to direct the surplus of American pilots by ones and twos into French Escadrilles. Altogether 212 Americans had enlisted in the Lafayette Corps before the declaration of war, the greater part of whom were still training in our schools.

CHAPTER VII

Battle of Flanders—Return to Verdun—Lufbery—Beauties of life in the air

Suddenly on the 17th of July, a new change of scene. This time it was right to the other end of the front, in Flanders, that we were to go. What was to happen there?

The pilots were delighted. "We're going to the sea-side," they said, and sure enough our field was right by the North Sea, a mile and a half south of Dunkirk, at a village called Saint-Pol-sur-Mer.

We had no map to go there, so I gave the young pilots a simple method of find their way. "Just follow the battle line, keeping it on the right as far as Nieuport, that is to the sea; you will easily distinguish the trenches, the shell-holes and the rows of 'sausages.' You cannot make a mistake. When you reach Nieuport, follow the coast backwards on your left until you reach a town—Dunkirk." None of them went wrong, but Doolittle, whose first flight with us it was, lost sight of his companions and tackled two enemy planes, who were assailing an English "sausage." He was brought down by them slightly wounded in the face. On our way we flew over Péronne and Bapaume, which were entirely destroyed. The region between them was everywhere pitted with shell-holes, not a spot anywhere to land in throughout this zone twenty-five miles long and thirteen wide. The country was a desert and the rich soil of Picardy was itself destroyed forever.

We perceived yet another martyred city—Arras. Its mutilated belfry was still standing proudly under the fire of the enemy guns. We passed over Vimy on whose famous ridge so much French and British blood had been spilt, then across Béthune, whose many chimneys were belching black smoke. Brave miners worked there day and night, even going far under the enemy's lines to extract from the only mines left to us the precious coal so needful for our industries. When these miners came up from their pits they were forced to put on masks against the gas bombardments, which the Germans daily opened against them. They were true soldiers, those miners.

On leaving Béthune—our Spads fly quickly— some of us made directly for Dunkirk via Cassel, perched curiously on the summit of its peak, while the rest flew in a curve over the hills of Flanders, the Red Hill, the Black Hill, and Kemmel, where the following year the German drive was to be arrested. Then past Messines, Ypres, dead city levelled with the ground, Dixmude, the Yser and its floods of famous memory, Nieuport and then back along the coast to the aerodrome. With the exception of Doolittle, every one landed successfully on the sandy-field of Saint Pol; tents were rapidly put up, which formed a delightful summer camp in the fine weather that prevailed.

Always while waiting for an attack there were a few days' respite, during which the intending assailant took care to show his aviation as little as possible and we pilots had consequently a brief period of rest. We naturally profited by the proximity of the sea to bathe a great deal. On this occasion my dog Fram showed once more his real intelligence. I had undressed on the sand and told him to watch my clothes while I was in the water some two hundred yards away. The tide was rising and was about to reach my uniform when to our amazement we saw the dog pick my clothes up in his jaws piece by piece and carry them up the shore well out of harm's way. All that without any orders, the clever fellow!

After the bath we used to fish with big nets and our mess was plentifully supplied with fish and shrimps. Thaw went in for boat-building —at least he wanted to construct a raft with a sail. He had bought some old barrels and some planks and hammered away all one day. Unfortunately the night was stormy and his raft was smashed before he had time to finish it to everybody's regret.

Naturally my pilots played base-ball also. Surely every good American takes with him as absolutely necessary baggage a bat, gloves, and some balls.

Some Canadians challenged us and inflicted a serious defeat upon us. I suppose the Giants or the Cubs would have defended the honour of the United States better than we did, as to make

up the team, which was one man short, I played
myself for the first time in my life. That fact
alone gives one an idea of the quality of our performance.

Dunkirk, an important sea-port, was moreover
a very pleasant and well supplied town. Moni-
tors were on guard before its harbour. They
were able to float in such shallow water that the
Boche submarines couldn't get in to torpedo them.

Throughout the day there was a continual going and coming of ships bringing shells and supplies from England, following the protected chan-
nel along the coast.

We were on the best of terms with our English
and Belgian comrades and paid each other many
visits. The British sailors often came to see us,
and I remember two receptions offered us by the
officers of the Coastal Motor Boats. These officers used to sally forth with only one seaman
as crew in little power boats, armed with a single torpedo. Every night they cruised up and
down before Ostende and Zeebrugge waiting a
chance to pull off a good coup. A hard life, but
one which they passionately enjoyed. Their existence on these little craft was no safer than on

our aeroplanes with which it had many points in common, which perhaps accounted for the sympathy between us.

Belgium was not far off, at least all of it that was left. The Royal family lived at La Panne, a seaside place where before the war people of moderate means, who could not afford the luxury of Ostend, used to spend the holidays. That heroic soldier, the King, was often there. One day we went there to get some supplies, especially sugar and tobacco. On our return Soubiran conceived the idea of telling the pilots who had stayed at home that we had met the King, that we had been introduced by a Belgian officer, and that the Sovereign had promised to visit the Escadrille to see the lions which interested him very much and decorate with his own hand all the pilots who had not yet received decorations. This yarn was believed and the young pilots impatiently awaited the Royal visit, while the Mess President made elaborate preparations to give the Royal guest a worthy reception.

How we laughed when the joke was exploded. I hope King Albert will pardon us.

As training while awaiting the offensive, we

threw bombs attached under our monoplanes at
floating buoys. We let them fall by means of
a lever after having dived straight down upon
the target. Our superiors intended to make us
execute a great offensive operation against the
enemy aerodromes on the morning of the attack
to destroy all the machines still in their nests
right at the outset. We were supposed to let
fall our bombs from a very low altitude, less
than 150 feet from the soil, to set on fire and
destroy the hangars, then fire our machine guns
at every machine which might try to come out
or fly away, and knock over mechanics and pilots
like ninepins. Machines were set aside to protect the operation at different altitudes and others
to attack all anti-aircraft defenses from a very
low position.

Often operations of this kind, in which the
English were past-masters, succeeded perfectly.
Once a single Spad set on fire four enemy planes
before they could leave the ground, but on the
31st of July, the day the offensive began, there
also started a veritable deluge, which no one who
fought in Flanders that year will ever forget.
Compared to it Noah's celebrated flood was only

a passing shower. All the aerial operations were greatly curtailed in consequence.

The offensive itself was not a little hampered. The first day the ground was still comparatively hard and a fine advance was made up to the outskirts of Houthulst forest. But in this spongy soil, where the water oozed through very rapidly and made any trench work impossible, what we wanted was exceptionally dry weather.

As it was there was no possibility of transporting munitions and food or of digging shelters. Trenches had to be made above the ground with sacks of earth built up and consequently both visible and easy to destroy.

The offensive stopped automatically despite its brilliant début. During the glimpses of fine weather all the aviation services, French, English and Belgian, were out at once to put them to the best advantage. On the other side the Richthofen circus was on the job. There were fantastic mêlées over Roulers, the Allies being distinctly superior. There was great rivalry amongst them, but Guynemer was far ahead of every one.

Besides the Boche there was considerable dan-

Zeppelin falling in flames struck by French artillerie at Compiégne March 17, 1917

Zeppelin brought down at Compiégne.

During the advance Nesles March 1917.

ger of being attacked by an Ally. There were lots
of novice pilots and a great diversity of machines,
so that this happened quite frequently; it is
much more difficult than the public imagines to
distinguish friend from foe in the air.

Our greatest Ace, whom I have just mentioned,
was once so attacked by an Allied novice, and
only managed to get rid of him by landing after
various manœuvres. His assailant, who by this
time had realized his mistake, did the same and
hurried up to apologize. Guynemer replied
curtly: "If I'd thought myself in danger there
would have been only one thing for me to do—
to bring you down." The other looked rather
sick, but I need hardly say that the whole thing
ended happily over a cup of tea.

On coming back from a patrol every one before landing used to perform the wildest aerial
acrobatics over his field. The English declined
to appear inferior in "stunting" to the French,
but I think I can truthfully say that thanks to
their Spad, which was in every way superior to
the English Sopwith triplane, the French were
decidedly ahead in this game.

Moreover, it is the French who invented "stunt"

flying. Several years before the war, on a tour through the United States, Garros, Audemars and Simon put up some remarkable performances in this line. Pégoud was the creator of the loop and most of the other stunts were perfected by Navarre, especially the spin. All these tricks were codified and taught to all the pilots in the war by Simon, who, as Captain Instructor at the Pau school, trained several thousand fighting pilots, so the French had a longer experience behind them.

By night the bombing Voisins, who shared our field, used to go out to work in their turn. Their great enemy was the fog, which rises very suddenly at the seaside. In the daytime fog is already a great danger for the airman, especially when it hangs very low. If the pilot gets caught in it, he doesn't know where he is going and is unable even to tell what is the position of his machine. At 125 miles an hour he is liable to crash against the first obstacle that he meets without even knowing it is there.

By day one can see fog banks far off on the horizon and land before going into them, but by night it is difficult to land anywhere else but on a field that has been provided with abundant lights.

One night, while our Voisins were away, the fog rose and covered the field. The searchlights and flares nevertheless indicated its situation by their light that was diffused through the fog so as to be visible from above, as the deadly curtain was of no great thickness. It was, however, bad enough to be altogether opaque to the eyes of the pilots and so when the Voisins came back they collected above the field and flew round, over the fog bank, in the hope that a welcome gust of wind would blow it away.

One after the other the machines plunged into the milky bank, then darted up again immediately, shaving the hangars. It was a terribly anxious time for us who could hear the hum of their motors above our heads and appreciate their danger. For them it must have been a frightful experience. Their gasoline gave out and one by one they had to take the chance of landing through the fatal bank. Everyone of them crashed on landing through judging the distance wrongly. Fortunately, no one was killed though there were many wounded, but I am sure that all those pilots will remember that raid for many a long day.

We were not destined to stay long at Dunkirk as the Flanders offensive was discontinued on account of the bad weather. In war it is no good being obstinate and if a thing fails it should be abandoned immediately and another blow prepared elsewhere. What was the result of the German stubbornness before Verdun in 1916 save to cut into pieces six hundred thousand of their men without any advantage to show for it?

As it happened the French High Command was preparing a new offensive at this very Verdun, where calm had reigned for a considerable length of time. We were naturally invited to take part in the show as we were in all of them, for Headquarters employed the Lafayette Escadrille just as it did the crack French units—no mean tribute to our American pilots.

Our new field was 250 miles away, but our Spads could cover this distance in less than two hours. Immediately on receipt of the order, we went off the 11th of August to Senart, a village situated just on the southern edge of the Argonne

forest near the source of the Aisne. After the
sea the forest—what more could we ask? A
piece of good news was awaiting us there; three
months before the Escadrille had been proposed
for a citation in Army Orders by Commander
Féquant, Head of our Group, and he was pleased
to inform us that the General in Chief, Pétain,
had just granted it. Here is the text of the citation:

"Order of General Headquarters No. 17946
August 15th, Escadrille No. 124 (Lafayette).

"Escadrille composed of American volunteers
who have come to fight for France in the purest
spirit of sacrifice. Has carried on ceaselessly,
under the command of Captain Thenault, an
ardent struggle against our enemies.

"In very heavy fighting and at the cost of serious losses, which far from weakening it, exalted
its morale, has brought down 28 enemy planes.

"Has roused the deep admiration of the chiefs,
who have had it under their orders, and of French
Escadrilles, which, fighting beside it, have wished
to rival its courage."

We had no need of this official testimonial to stimulate us, but we were about to find ourselves in the hardest sector we had ever flown over.

A great part of the German aviation from Flanders had preceded us to this new sector. It is true that as a result of the concave form of the front the Germans had only the chord of the arc to fly across, while we had the arc itself. The Germans were generally forewarned of all our offensives by the great concentrations of artillery which then preceded every attack. Even if they hadn't seen the assembled batteries they could not have failed to be enlightened by the thunderous din of the preparation.

In 1917 an attack never took place without at least three days of "drum fire." Whereas in 1918, after the experience of the British at Cambrai with their tanks, artillery preparations only lasted two hours at the outside and were sometimes omitted altogether. The results were much better because thus there was surprise, a primordial factor of success.

We were pleased—which is one way of putting it—to meet again at Verdun our old acquaintances the "Tangos." This Boche formation was so-called because the body of its planes was painted the exact orange shade called tango. As they were there we had to meet them in good spirits which we did. They were among the most famous of the German flying men, and the game was fast and furious from the start. To get our hand in we began by going to bomb them several days running, that is to say we protected the bombing machines. In the course of one of these expeditions Willis went down fighting bravely. It was a heavy loss for the Escadrille, for with his trained and intelligent brain he always brought back from his trips information that was greatly prized by the High Command. It is very hard to make good observations in a single-seater. Willis had made a specialty of it and thanks to the speed of his machine, he was able to go to places where the slower two-seaters could not have ventured without being brought down.

After several weeks of anxiety we learned that our friend was only prisoner and I was very glad to have written to his mother my hope that this was the case. She received my letter at almost the same time as the definite news from Germany.

"I am keeping your letter as one of my most precious jewels," she replied to me, "for I am happy to see from it that his superiors always considered him a man of character. I hope that as a prisoner my son will still serve his country."

During this war I have received numerous letters from American mothers. The attitude of these mothers was admirable, and their sentiment of sacrifice and self-forgetfulness was worthy of Cornelia the mother of the Gracchi.

Willis tried to escape and managed to succeed some time before the armistice by swimming across the Rhine.

At the same period, September, 1917, another American, who was flying with a French Escadrille in our Group, was brought down on one of his first outings. He was a desperate fighter.

After capture he determined to escape—no matter how. As a weapon he had only a clasp knife. During his flight four sentinels, one after the other, loosed on him their dogs, fired at him and missed. But he did not miss three of them, for

The Viaduct of Dannemarie destroyed by a bombardment of heavy calibre.

The effects of a heavy calibre shell.

How the bombs were placed and let fall.

Assembly for orders before leaving on first patrol. No emotion visible.

with the aid of darkness he cut the throats of all
three.   Think of his fate if he had been recap-
tured!   But he was determined to come back and
fight at all costs, for he felt that he had not yet
done enough.   How could Germany hope to conquer men like that?

But to return to our "friends" the Tangos.

In the September sky, whose blue was softened
by the gentle and misty white, how fine and thrilling was the meeting of two patrols.   First the
ruse in approaching; each one trying to get the
sun behind him so as to blind the opponent;
then the decision to attack which once taken made
you forget everything else.   A tiger leaping on
its defenceless prey, an eagle swooping on a timid
hare, cannot have more confidence in their own
strength than the pilot who grasps his controls
with firm hands and fixing his eye on the sight of
his machine gun to calculate the corrections to
be made, aims at a certain part of the enemy's
machine and coolly lets death loose by pulling his
little lever.   Yet those are seconds of emotion
which are well worth living.   Compared to that,
hunting the royal tiger or the grizzly bear is but
child's play.   It is life in its greatest intensity

when you see your adversary smitten with his death blow, falling to join the dust of the earth, like a shot pheasant, which falls head downward through the air. And when the two opponents, each having missed the other, try to dodge one another in an infernal whirl, each one describing circles more and more narrow so as to catch the other in his field of fire, and when more skilful you are master of the situation and force the enemy to headlong flight, even if you have not succeeded in bringing him down, your motor sings clear in the heavens and there is a note of triumph in its purr. You forget for a moment all the dangers that lurk in the blue sky, you forget those who have fallen or that a moment hence you may fall in your turn.

No, you think only of your work because you are a man, because there is an enemy, and because you must beat him.

Certainly the pilot without suspecting it possesses at this moment the same mentality as the cave man defending himself and his family with a club against the attacks of wild beasts. And I prefer this simple and brutal mentality to that

which is too often produced by centuries of so-
called civilization.

Moreover, you are in the space of heaven, you
climb to dizzy heights and the power of your
motor frees you from weight, which is always
like a ball chained to the foot of other mortals.
You can descend with the greatest ease at the
undreamt and unheard of speed of 250 miles an
hour. Falls of 3000 feet are nothing. The air
itself is an amazing shock absorber, and its
depths are there to receive you more gently than
the net breaks the thirty foot fall of a tight-rope
dancer. The two hundred and fifty horses of
your engine obey the lightest pressure of your
fingers or your most trifling whim. You are
their master and in addition to the joys of flying
you taste the joys of victory.

It is easy to understand that hundreds of men
became passionately devoted to this superterres-
trial existence and gave up all to it, even their
lives.

The Tangos might come. With their brave
comrades of the French army the pilots of the
Lafayette Escadrille were there. High up in the

sunlight, tiny motes shone, dived and manœuvred. They were men, sitting on machines of wood and canvas. The machine guns uttered the savage tic-tac of their deadly song. The incendiary bullets of the Germans left in the air great white trails, phosphorous bullets they were, whose poisoned wounds were always mortal—an unpleasant thing to remember when you saw them pass through your planes. One had to defend one's self and the best fashion of defence, is it not attack? So we attacked.

Above all the pilots who found themselves at Verdun was Lufbery "without fear and without reproach" like Bayard the loyal knight of Garigliano bridge. His Spad was always the highest and every day he won new victories. He seemed to hardly care about having them confirmed. Calmly he reigned as sovereign lord in his chosen element and beat down his foes to accomplish his duty and not for the sake of glory.

It was worth seeing him appear above the forest of Argonne and come down into our green meadow, bordered by the tall poplars which rise beside the river Aisne.

Each pilot can be recognized by his flight, but

Lufbery stood out by the mastery and ease with which he executed his daring renversements and all the acrobatic stunts. Almost all pilots can perform them mechanically, but only the real artists can perform them gently and without roughness so as not to bring any abnormal strain upon the planes of the machine. Lufbery always landed with the greatest skill. He never harmed his machine, but, on the other hand, one could often mark on it the savage traces of battles in which it had been engaged.

He made his report very briefly and when the occasion offered used to paint, smiling broadly, a tiny red bar on one of the struts of his plane to indicate a new victory.

His simplicity was remarkable. During his leisure hours he used to work with the mechanics, who adored him, in perfecting details of his machine and machine-gun. When everything was ready, his greatest joy was to go off with some comrades across country. He had been educated in France in the province of Auvergne before going off around the world, and he knew what was to be found in our fields as in those of other countries. He would often bring back game or mushrooms which gave the cook a chance to vary our menu. One of his favourite amusements was to go and play with the lions which he had adopted. In response the lions adopted him as master and recognized him amongst all of us. It was a sight to see the brave Whiskey, when he spotted Lufbery, hurl himself upon him at full gallop as if to devour him, but it was to devour him with caresses—the caresses of a lion who can hide his terrible claws so as not to harm his friends. Lufbery was the only one for whom Soda was good and gentle. Was not that the proof of a great personal power that even the wild beasts should appreciate his influence?

When it was fine Lufbery at once busied himself with his machine and took it out for a voluntary patrol. He had to be given positive orders to keep him from being always in the air. To fly high is very fatiguing as the sudden changes of altitude quickly tire the heart. But never have I met a pilot with more endurance than Lufbery. When the sky was clear he would go up three or four times a day to eighteen thousand feet just for his own pleasure, in a dilettante fashion.

Never was he at all ill from it.   He was a super-
man. . . .

The Tangos were only men and Lufbery gave
them a hard life.

This second battle of Verdun was, as everyone
knows, a wonderful success.   Although the enemy
was expecting it the attack was carried out with
so much dash that Hill 304, the Mort Homme
and its tunnels, were all retaken in a single drive
and in the same shock thousands of prisoners
fell into our hands with hundreds of guns.

The reaction was sharp, especially on the right
bank of the Meuse.   With devilish ingenuity the
Boches had just invented or rather begun to util-
ize a new toxic gas that was really terrible.

I refer to Yperite or mustard gas.   This gas
spread by means of shells, was greatly dreaded
on account of the long time it hung about and
the ease with which it impregnated everything—
ground, huts, equipment, clothes, even the hair.

In contact with the skin it formed sulphuric
acid causing frightful burns, and if one was so
unfortunate as to breathe it the lungs shrivelled
up like old leather.   Death followed after ter-

rible suffering. Naturally our chemists quickly learned all about it and our factories began manufacturing it to such an extent that when the following year we gave it them back tenfold, our enemies had the incredible audacity to protest against its use.

Despite the Yperite our troops held firm, though they had to wear their masks all the time, which the great heat rendered very uncomfortable.

We, aviators, had no time to waste. Apart from fighting proper, that is the destruction of enemy's aviation, we had had before the attack to ensure the protection of bombing squadrons far behind the enemy's lines. And on days of attack we were expected to accompany the assaulting waves, searching out with our machine guns the ripples of ground where reserves might be hiding and hurling light bombs upon them. We had too in some cases to go and verify information, or even take photographs with an automatic apparatus. Willis in Flanders brought back some very interesting photographs with his single-seater.

To protect their machines the Escadrilles of

Farman Bomb Plane.

Farman Bomb Plane

A Nieuport in full flight.

A Nieuport in friendly combat with a Farman.

artillery aviation often asked us to act as guards. For this work no fighting Escadrille was more sought after than our own. That was very complimentary. The sheep were always delighted with their watch-dogs and that is a proof that the wolves were kept at a distance.

One day, during one of these protective missions in charge of Lt. de Maison Rouge, de Laage's successor, our patrol brought down an enemy plane which was trying to attack a machine protected by us. Peterson distinguished himself in this battle which was fought just above Montfaucon, the famous hill of which we were trying to get a photograph. A year later the American army was to carry this historic hill brilliantly by assault.

That gallant and excellent pilot Bridgman also did very good work during this whole period, never sparing himself in the slightest. On one occasion Lufbery saved the life of Parsons and myself by protecting us from a Tango which we hadn't seen, as its approach was hidden from view by our planes. Just as he was about to attack us, Lufbery, whom I always placed above the patrol to dominate the situation, dived suddenly, which woke my attention and I perceived the intruder. What a hunt followed over Forges Wood! He escaped us by diving so sharply that I was surprised not to see his wings give way, as sometimes happened with their Albatros. The Spad was the only machine which enabled one to dive without fear of the consequences and often in diving on an enemy plane, which in turn dived to escape, one had the pleasant surprise of seeing it come to pieces in the air without a shot having been fired.

At this time a piece of sad news, at first whispered and which no one would believe, spread over the front; Guynemer was missing on the 11th of September. The Germans, however, made no mention of the fact. If they had known it there is not the least doubt that their radios would have announced the fact throughout the world as a brilliant victory. For it was one indeed. . . .

We liked to think of him as invincible, and yet when one came to think of it, was it not rather natural to feel that that was the fate which awaited all fighting pilots? Boelke and Immerman, the German Aces, had been brought down by quite inexperienced adversaries.

Two average pilots have an equal chance of winning. It's just a toss up and luck can't hold for ever. A spent bullet, fired by an unskilled hand is often enough. Think of the superhuman skill which Lufbery required to reach his score and a half of victories (counting those that were not officially confirmed) or of Guynemer to get long past fifty, and Fonck, who the following year, was to get close to the hundred without ever being touched.[1]

It was only a long time after his disappearance that it was learned that Guynemer had fallen in mysterious circumstances near Poelcapelle in Flanders. The bombardment in that region was so intense that never a trace of his aeroplane was found.

The greatest amongst us had fallen, but there were many fired by his example eager and ready to follow in the Master's footsteps.

[1] Fonck had a special trick of getting position to fire . . . a trick that was very difficult to apply and only to be accomplished by an exceptional pilot. He fired at his victims from an angle of 75° ahead and above them, out of their field of fire. To apply a method like this one needed to have a mastery in flight that was absolutely unrivalled.

All September there was very hard fighting. Bigelow was wounded at the end of August by a bullet in the face and left us. Even our nights were very agitated. We were still on the same field as a group of night bombers, which is a thing to avoid if possible because their searchlights are bound to attract the riposte of the enemy's bombing squadrons. The latter attacked us furiously and not only us but the hospitals in the neighbourhood, for instance that of Vadelaincourt, where doctors and nurses were killed beside the wounded over whom they were working. But it was against us that the enemy came for preference, paying us several visits. On the first occasion, the 25th of September, there was little damage done, but two days later they came back in great force. Thaw and Lufbery fired a machine gun from the ground against these unwelcome visitors. They were using tracer bullets and in other circumstances the firework effect would have been delightful to watch. The enemy machines came regularly over one after the other at intervals of a quarter of an hour at a very low altitude. When their bombs fell the ground shook at the terrific force of the explosion. My pilots and I were sheltering in an open trench and one should have heard the jokes with which Hall kept up the spirits of his comrades at each explosion. The classic joke, reserved for occasions when the situation became, shall we say, rather tiresome, was to ask recently-joined pilots "Are you glad, boy, you've joined the army?" Pronounced with an inimitable twang this phrase always had a great success. In the midst of our laughter the enemy bullets whistled over our heads, for his airmen had set fire to one of our hangars and were shooting up the blaze to prevent us from extinguishing it.

My mechanic, Michel Plaaporte, formerly working with Norman Prince, tried heroically to prevent the fire from spreading, and the artillery work of Thaw and Lufbery, despite the fact that they were firing haphazard as they could see nothing, was not without results, for the next morning we found on the field a Boche map and airman's helmet all stained with blood. Their owner had certainly not got away unscathed. The destruction of our planes by this fire didn't have serious consequences for at this time we could get as many as we wanted. I sent all the pilots who had lost machines to get new ones in Paris. That was some consolation for them.

On the 24th of September the brave MacMonagle was killed in a fight by a bullet through the head. He fell in the forest of Hesse between the Argonne and Verdun. Mrs. MacMonagle, his mother, a really devoted war worker, was informed. She left for a moment the work of aid for wounded soldiers, which she was carrying on in Paris with such great devotion, and came to accompany her son to his last resting place. He was buried at Triaucourt.

For the first time American soldiers, engineers working on a neighbouring railroad acted as guard of honour and fired the last salute over his grave. An American band played the funeral dirge. MacMonagle had fallen but America was coming.

At Verdun one hundred and fifty hard fights were fought by the Lafayette Escadrille, but we could only manage to get five victories confirmed. We had one pilot killed, one wounded and one taken prisoner; the advantage was still on our side.

Headquarters had not yet done with us for this year. We had to make yet another change of camp. It was without regret that we left our summer encampment, for the bad weather would be upon us in a month. We returned to our former field at Chaudun.

CHAPTER VIII

Return to Chaudun—Trip to Champagne—Transfer of
the Escadrille to the American Army—Farewell

This time our duty was to take part in the Malmaison offensive and the recapture of the whole
Chemin des Dames, the offensive of October
10th, which was wonderfully successful. More
than 10,000 prisoners and hundreds of guns were
captured. I was ill and had to leave the Escadrille for a month, during which time Thaw took
my place.

Lieutenant Verdier-Fauvety had replaced
Lieutenant de Maison Rouge and had rapidly
won the affection of the American pilots and
given me the most valuable assistance. He had
just escaped death in the most remarkable manner. At 10,000 feet altitude he had collided with
another Spad and the two damaged planes fell
in a spin from which they were unable to recover.

After the bombardment.

After the bombardment.

German machine brought down near the second line.

German machine brought down by Lufbery.

By extraordinary luck both he and his comrade came down on some trees and both got off with trifling injuries. The following year he died fighting bravely while in command of an Escadrille. De Maison Rouge met the same fate. During the preparation for the offensive the daring Campbell was killed in a fight over the famous Ailette reservoir. He fell into a marsh and was buried at Pargny by the Germans. Jones, who had taken part in the fight, came back with three of his control wires cut by bullets; he had had a narrow escape. About this time James Hall, recovered from his wound, rejoined the Escadrille.

The first day of the attack Lufbery brought down six enemy machines. Unfortunately they could not all be confirmed as the infantry was in full movement and the control services were naturally somewhat disorganized in consequence. They had other work to do. However, several French aviators supplied unofficial confirmation. Lufbery was at this time in marvelous form.

Thaw, Verdier, James Hall, Peterson, Bridgman, Parsons, Marr, Soubiran, Dugan, Jones, etc., continued to do excellent work. They attacked the enemy "sausages" frequently and set a number of them on fire.

The battle continued throughout October. Ford came to join the Escadrille, the last recruit we were to receive. November was calm on account of the weather and incessant fogs. We took advantage of it to pay frequent visits to the pleasant Hotel de la Chasse at Villers-Cotterets.

It was then that Commander Féquant getting anxious at the size of our lions—for Whiskey was now bigger than a very large Great Dane—ordered us to get rid of them. He permitted us to take them to the Zoological Garden in Paris, to which we had already determined to give them when the time came. At present (June, 1919), Whiskey is still there though suffering greatly from rheumatism contracted during the severe winter of 1916 on the Somme, where he shared our draughty sheds. I went to see him and though he recognized and came to the front of the cage to lick my hand, he seemed to be suffering a great deal, and I am afraid that he will not long survive his companion Soda who died of the same ailment.

We were very sad to think that we were losing

our mascots and to see them condemned to imprisonment for life. Whiskey gave us no trouble on the trip to Paris, but Soda, whom by the way we had never succeeded in taming to the same extent as her companion, behaved badly, showing ill temper just when one expected it least and when she reached Paris refused to come out of her box to enter the cage where she was to pass the rest of her days.

She fell into a furious passion and as she could easily have torn a hand off any of us we didn't insist and put off the business of transferring her until the morrow.

Why was it that Soda was always much worse-tempered than good old Whiskey? . . . Insoluble mystery of the caprices of the feminine soul. . . .

On December 2nd Lufbery brought down two planes one after the other, thus celebrating the anniversary of the Battle of Austerlitz.

On the following day Headquarters sent us to Champagne, where the Boche by immense camouflage preparation gave the impression they were about to attack.

We established ourselves at La Noblette, north

of Chalons. The Escadrille Lafayette No. 124 had thus covered the whole front and every sector.

The weather began to be very cold and our sheds were open to the wind and the snow. Luckily Chalons was quite close and we could easily get supplies. Perhaps on account of the cold, which always gave a lot of trouble with the lubrication, there was a considerable lull in aerial activity.

The moment of transfer to the American army was drawing near and formed the subject of all our thoughts. It took place on January 1st, 1918, as arranged, and the Lafayette Escadrille became the first American fighting Escadrille with the number 103. It kept, however, its French mechanics and material. I left it with deep regrets and many pleasant memories.

This Escadrille was in turn the nucleus of a fighting group, the first, which was formed almost immediately and of which Thaw remained in charge. Lufbery went off to organize another and some months later, setting as always the example, met a glorious death in battle. He fell in Lorraine near Toul. There died there a very

Baby Nieuport armed with Lewis gun firing over the propeller.

Country in Alsace—Thann Valley.

An aviation field in Alsace. — Romagny.

Machine destroyed by storm (May 1916).

wonderful personality and his death was an incalculable loss to the Allies. His friends will never cease to regret him.

In 1918 the Aviation of the United States became strongly organized and at the armistice it had reached the imposing proportions that all the world knows. The Lafayette Escadrille was largely drawn upon to organize these new forces. All the pilots became Commanders of Escadrilles and gave their younger comrades the benefit of their experience. By the force of their example new Aces were to appear.

But my task is finished and I leave to others the work of following them through these new battlefields. In these pages I have tried to give a faithful account of this nucleus of the great American air fleet, and to show the noble sentiments which had brought these pioneers amongst us long before the brutality of facts had moved the unanimous feeling of the nation. It will be the honour of my life to have commanded them.

Let us bow low before them and salute them very respectfully. Glory to all these volunteers. Glory to all these noble heroes, these noble forerunners. The Nation which bore them is a great nation, and I am sure that Remembrance will keep fresh their names and teach their deeds to its children and children's children.

To my former comrades in arms, to all those who have fallen, I can give the assurance that despite her sufferings France will never forget them in her eternal gratitude.

List of pilots who served in the Lafayette Escadrille from its formation April 16, 1916, until the day when it was transferred to the American Army (January 1, 1918).

THENAULT, Georges, Captain commanding the Escadrille	(12/ 4/16)	(1/ 1/18)
De LAAGE De MEUX	(16/ 4/16)	(23/ 5/17)
CHAPMAN, Victor	(20/ 4/16)	(24/ 5/16)
PRINCE, Norman	(20/ 4/16)	(14/ 9/16)
MAC CONNELL, James	(20/ 4/16)	(19/ 3/17)
ROCKWELL, Kiffin	(20/ 4/16)	(23/ 9/16)
THAW, William	(28/ 4/16)	(1/ 1/18)
HALL, Bert	(28/ 4/16)	(10/11/16)
COWDIN, Elliot	(28/ 4/16)	(25/ 6/16)
RUMSEY, Laurence	(4/ 6/16)	(25/11/16)
BALSLEY, H.	(28/ 5/16)	(19/ 6/16)
LUFBERY, Raoul	(24/ 5/16)	(1/ 1/18)
JOHNSON, Charles	(28/ 5/16)	(15/ 4/17)
HILL, Dudley	(9/ 6/16)	(1/ 1/18)
MASSON, Didier	(19/ 6/16)	(30/ 1/17)
PAVELKA, Paul	(10/ 8/16)	(24/ 1/17)
ROCKWELL, Robert	(17/ 9/16)	(1/ 1/18)
PRINCE, Frederic	(22/10/16)	(14/ 1/17)
SOUBIRAN, Robert	(22/10/16)	(1/ 1/18)
HAVILAND, Willis	(22/10/16)	(2/ 9/17)
HOSKIER, Ronald Wood	(14/12/16)	(23/ 4/17)
GENET, Edmond	(19/ 1/17)	(17/ 4/17)
PARSONS, Edwin	(27/ 1/17)	(1/ 1/18)
BIGELOW, Stephen	(8/ 2/17)	(11/ 9/17)
WILLIS, Harold	(1/ 3/17)	(18/ 8/17)
HINKLE, Edward	(1/ 3/17)	(15/ 6/17)
LOWELL, Walter	(1/ 3/17)	(1/10/17)
HEWITT, Thomas	(30/ 3/17)	(14/ 9/17)
MARR, Kenneth	(30/ 3/17)	(1/ 1/18)
DUGAN, William	(30/ 3/17)	(1/ 1/18)
CAMPBELL, Andrew Courtney	(16/ 4/17)	(5/10/17)
BRIDGMAN, Ray	(2/ 5/17)	(1/ 1/18)
DREXEL, John	(12/ 5/17)	(21/ 7/17)
DOLAN, Charles	(12/ 5/17)	(1/ 1/18)
JONES, Henri	(12/ 5/17)	(1/ 1/18)

DE MAISON-ROUGE, Arnoux .... (28/ 5/17)   (15/ 9/17)
PETERSON, David .... (12/ 6/17)   (1/ 1/18)
HALL, James .... (16/ 6/17)   (1/ 1/18)
MAC-MONAGLE, Douglas .... (15/ 6/17)   (24/ 9/17)
DOOLITTLE .... (3/ 7/17)   (17/ 7/17)
VERDIER-FAUVETY .... (6/10/17)   (1/ 1/18)
FORD, Christophe .... (7/11/19)   (1/ 1/18)

THE END